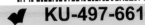
PREPARING YOURSELF

36 BELIEVING IN YOURSELF

38 ANALYZING APPEARANCE

40 ENHANCING BODY IMAGE

42 IMPROVING YOUR VOICE

44 ELIMINATING TENSION

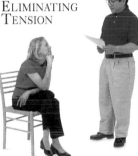

DELIVERING A PRESENTATION

46 CONTROLLING NERVES

50 SPEAKING CONFIDENTLY

54 CLOSING EFFECTIVELY

HANDLING AN AUDIENCE

56 JUDGING THE MOOD

60 DEALING WITH QUESTIONS

64 COPING WITH HOSTILITY

68 ASSESSING YOUR ABILITY

70 INDEX

72 ACKNOWLEDGMENTS

MAKING
PRESENTATIONS

TIM HINDLE

Lon

A DORLING KINDERSLEY BOOK

Project Editor Sasha Heseltine
Editor David Tombesi-Walton
Designers Elaine C. Monaghan,
Austin Barlow
Assistant Editor Felicity Crowe
Assistant Designer Laura Watson

DTP Designer Jason Little
Production Controller Alison Jones

Series Editor Jane Simmonds
Series Art Editor Jayne Jones

Managing Editor Stephanie Jackson
Managing Art Editor Nigel Duffield

First published in Great Britain in 1998
by Dorling Kindersley Limited,
9 Henrietta Street,
London WC2E 8PS

4 6 8 10 9 7 5

Copyright © 1998
Dorling Kindersley Limited, London
Text copyright © 1998 Tim Hindle

Visit us on the World Wide Web at
http://www.dk.com

A CIP catalogue record for this book is available
from the British Library

ISBN 0 7513 0527 8

Reproduced by Colourscan, Singapore
Printed in Hong Kong by Wing King Tong Co. Ltd.

CONTENTS

4 INTRODUCTION

PREPARING A PRESENTATION

6 DEFINING
YOUR PURPOSE

8 KNOWING
YOUR AUDIENCE

10 DEALING WITH
LOGISTICS

14 KNOWING
YOUR VENUE

18 CLARIFYING
OBJECTIVES

20 FINDING
MATERIAL

22 STRUCTURING
MATERIAL

26 WRITING A
PRESENTATION

30 USING AUDIO-
VISUAL AIDS

34 REHEARSING

INTRODUCTION

Whether you are a seasoned orator or a novice speaker, Making Presentations will help you to improve your presentation skills through planning, preparation, and performance. Techniques for speaking with confidence, choosing audio-visual aids, and dealing with questions from an audience, for example, are explained clearly to help you to develop your presenting skills. Practical advice is given to furnish you with the confidence you need to handle real-life situations professionally, while 101 concise tips scattered throughout the book give further vital information. Finally, a self-assessment exercise allows you to evaluate and chart your progress following each presentation you give. This book provides invaluable information that you will be able to utilize over and over again as your presenting skills develop.

PREPARING A PRESENTATION

There are two secrets to making a good presentation: preparation and practice. Take the time to prepare properly, and your chances of success will increase enormously.

DEFINING YOUR PURPOSE

What do you want to communicate to your audience? Before you start to prepare your presentation, decide what you want it to achieve. Focus on the purpose of the presentation at every stage to ensure that your preparation is relevant and efficient.

 1 Once you have written your speech, cut it, cut it, and cut it.

POINTS TO REMEMBER

- Your presentation should be relevant, simple, and to the point.

- Your audience will be impressed by the depth and breadth of your knowledge rather than a show of false intellect and wit.

- Your positive attitude, energy, and enthusiasm for the subject will speak volumes. They will be remembered by your audience long after the details of your speech have been forgotten.

CONSIDERING YOUR AIMS

The first points to think about are what you intend to tell your audience and how best to communicate your message. Your strategy will depend on three things: the type of message you wish to deliver; the nature of the audience; and the physical surroundings of the venue.

Review the purpose of your presentation, and ask yourself whether it is simple enough or too complex. Think about who might be in your audience and how they might receive your speech. Then ask yourself if this is how you want your speech to be received. If not, modify your purpose.

ASSESSING ABILITIES

Unless you are a trained actor, it is difficult trying to be anyone other than yourself. Concentrate on defining and utilizing your best assets. For example if you have a good, clear voice, use it to your advantage; if you have a talent for such things, tell a humorous but relevant short anecdote. Next, confront your fears and anxieties about the presentation, so that you can make sure that you are prepared for them on the day.

 Group similar ideas together to establish themes.

SPEAKING ▶ CONFIDENTLY
Use techniques that you are comfortable with in your presentation. This will help you control your nerves once you are standing in front of the audience.

REDUCING YOUR FEARS

COMMON FEARS	PRACTICAL SOLUTIONS
EXCESSIVE NERVES You cannot relax. You forget what you are trying to say and dry up.	Prepare by rehearsing in front of a mirror and, if possible, at the venue. Make sure that you can see your notes clearly at all times. Take a deep breath, and smile.
BORED AUDIENCE The audience loses interest, and fidget and talk among themselves.	Ensure that the point you are trying to make is relevant – if not, cut it. Be enthusiastic. Vary the pace of your presentation, and maintain eye contact with the audience.
HOSTILE AUDIENCE You are heckled. Questions from the floor are aggressive in tone.	Remain polite and courteous. If your audience has specialist knowledge of your subject, defer to them. Redirect difficult questions back to the audience.
BREAKDOWN OF VISUAL AIDS Equipment fails to work, or you cannot remember how to use it.	Avoid using any technology with which you are not thoroughly familiar. Immediately before the presentation, check all the equipment that you will be using.

KNOWING YOUR AUDIENCE

Find out as much as you can about who will be attending your presentation. Have you invited some of the audience? Does it consist of colleagues? Once you know who will be attending, structure your speech to elicit the best response from them.

3 Make sure that the audience leaves the venue feeling informed.

QUESTIONS TO ASK YOURSELF

Q What is the expected size of the audience?

Q What is the average age of the audience?

Q What is the ratio of males to females in the audience?

Q Is the audience well informed about your subject?

Q Has the audience chosen, or been asked, to attend?

Q What do the members of the audience have in common?

Q What prejudices does the audience hold?

Q What is the cultural make-up of the audience?

Q Does everyone or anyone in the audience know you?

4 Always remember to talk *to* your audience, rather than *at* them.

EVALUATING AN AUDIENCE

To communicate your message effectively, you need to take account of the cultural values and opinions held by your audience. Consider how they might react to any sensitive issues raised in your speech, and be aware that this could affect the rest of your presentation. If the audience members are known to hold strong opinions on your chosen subject, be wary of introducing contentious issues without supporting your point of view, and remember that humour can easily cause offence, so use it sparingly in your speech.

FINDING OUT MORE

The primary source of information about your audience will be the organizer of the event at which you are speaking. If your presentation is to be included as part of a conference, ask for a list of the delegates in advance. If you are making a presentation to a potential new client, ask your contacts in the appropriate industry what they can tell you about them. Before addressing a public meeting, take the time to read the local press to see what concerns your audience might have. Use this prior knowledge to your best advantage – a speech that connects directly with members of the audience and shows that you have done your background work will be well received.

Being Adaptable

The size of the audience will have a significant impact on the way you structure your presentation. With small groups there is plenty of opportunity for two-way interaction – you can answer questions as you go along, or you can ask your audience for their opinions about the questions and issues you are raising. With large groups, the communication is almost entirely one-way, and a very different approach is required by the speaker. It is vital that your material is clear, precise, and easy to follow so that the audience's interest is held throughout.

5 Involve your audience in the presentation as much as possible.

Adjusting Your Presentation to Audience Size

Audience Size	Presentation Styles	Techniques
Small Audience A group of fewer than 15 people is considered a small audience. Most people will be asked to address an audience of this size at some point in their working career.	**Formal** Follow formal procedures in committee meetings, sales pitches to prospective clients, and interdepartmental presentations.	● Establish eye contact with each member of the group at an early stage. ● Face your audience at all times – this will help hold their attention.
	Informal Use informality to break the ice when presenting new products to known suppliers and when presenting to colleagues.	● Interact with the audience by soliciting questions. ● Allow individuals to have a say, but keep it brief.
Large Audience A group of 15 or more people constitutes a large audience. It is easier to address this size of audience if you already have previous presenting experience. 	**Formal** Follow formal procedures when giving a speech at a conference or at the annual general meeting of a public company.	● Make sure that all of the audience members are able to hear you clearly, especially at the back of the venue. ● Link, sum up, emphasize, and repeat main points.
	Informal Use informal procedures when making a spontaneous presentation from the floor at a formal conference.	● Speak slowly, and enunciate at all times. ● Keep your message broad, general, and simple. Go into more detail only if asked.

DEALING WITH LOGISTICS

Only meticulous organization can ensure that your presentation will be effective. Careful planning of the practical details in advance will free you nearer the time to concentrate on perfecting your presentation, rather than dealing with unforeseen hitches.

6 Visit the venue in advance to become familiar with its layout.

CONSIDERING KEY POINTS AT THE START

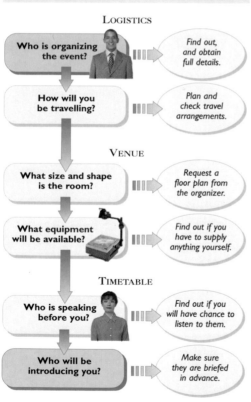

LOGISTICS

Who is organizing the event? → *Find out, and obtain full details.*

How will you be travelling? → *Plan and check travel arrangements.*

VENUE

What size and shape is the room? → *Request a floor plan from the organizer.*

What equipment will be available? → *Find out if you have to supply anything yourself.*

TIMETABLE

Who is speaking before you? → *Find out if you will have chance to listen to them.*

Who will be introducing you? → *Make sure they are briefed in advance.*

ORGANIZING YOUR SCHEDULE

At an early stage, think through the event in its entirety. If the venue being used is not local, you will need to plan your travel arrangements and organize accommodation well in advance. Try to allow about three hours on the day of the presentation, or the evening before, to prepare yourself for it – both mentally and physically. You should also set aside about an hour to think through your speech and, if possible, rehearse on arrival at the venue. Plan what clothes to wear, and ensure they are clean and pressed. If you are the first (or only) speaker, check that any equipment you will be using is in working order.

7 Compile a schedule of preparations for the day.

PLANNING TRAVEL

Calculate your departure time carefully to avoid arriving late at your venue and not having sufficient time to prepare. Work backwards from the time you want to arrive, adding together journey times, then add at least one hour as a safety factor. Allow for delays, and if travelling by plane, include the time of the journey from the airport. Build enough time into your schedule to rest, and to overcome jet-lag if you are travelling over a long distance to give your speech.

8 Take work with you to occupy journey time.

ANALYZING TRAVEL REQUIREMENTS

Where is the event taking place?
Try to combine it with another visit nearby.

How are you travelling?
Obtain any medication you need for travel sickness.

Do you need to allow for jet-lag?

How long will the journey take?
Make an effort to use the time effectively.

Will you need to find accommodation?
Make arrangements for expenses.

MAKING TIME TO PREPARE

The casual, seemingly effortless presentations that are most successful are invariably the result of a great deal of preparation, research, and hard work. A company chairperson's annual speech to shareholders may take several speechwriters weeks of drafting and redrafting before it is of a suitable standard, whereas an induction for new trainees may take considerable work initially but then require only a little last-minute reworking. Start preparing at least four weeks before your presentation to allow time to formulate ideas and gather any necessary reference material. As you gain experience, you may find that you need less time.

9 For every hour of presentation, put aside 10 hours for preparation.

MAKING ITINERARIES AND CHECKLISTS

Even the most organized speakers have many practicalities to remember before giving a speech. Making an itinerary and listing all the materials and props that you require for your presentation are as essential to preparation as rehearsing your speech. The safest way to do this is to make a checklist, noting down points as you think of them. Work through your checklist, and try to foresee any potential hitches. If the presentation is taking place away from your place of work, make sure that you leave a contact number with your colleagues in case they need to get in touch with you during the day. Be sure they know the time of the presentation, and ask them not to disturb you just before or during it – except in a real emergency.

10 Confirm all the details of the event in writing with the organizers.

11 Always check the expertise of guest speakers carefully.

POINTS TO REMEMBER

- Potential venues should always be checked out for suitability.
- Size of audience plays a crucial role in the choice of venue.
- In most cases, personal opinions should not influence choice of guest speakers.
- A list of alternative speakers should be made in case your first choice cannot attend.
- Whenever possible, professional rivalries between guest speakers need to be avoided.
- Direct questions or comments from members of the audience should always be channelled through the chairperson.
- Details of dates, venues, order of proceedings, and other speakers must be circulated in advance.

ORGANIZING A PRESENTATION YOURSELF

If you are asked to organize a presentation yourself, there are several important decisions to make early on concerning the venue, speakers, and size of audience. Draw up a list of possible venues to compare the advantages and disadvantages of each, bearing in mind costs, location, capacity, and facilities. Select a venue to suit the size of your audience and the style of the presentation. Pass on all these details to the other speakers so that they can organize their presentations accordingly. Keep an alternative venue in mind in case your first choice is not available on the date you require or falls through after it has been booked. When considering guest speakers, check their credentials thoroughly to ensure that they have the necessary expertise. Give them plenty of notice, and reconfirm the details before the presentation. As with venues, keep alternative speakers in mind.

ORGANIZING A GROUP PRESENTATION

If you are going to organize a group presentation, you need to consider some additional points. The secret of a successful group presentation is to keep a tight hold on the proceedings, since events can easily degenerate into chaos if people speak out of turn. Discuss beforehand the order in which the panel members will speak, and draw up an agenda well in advance so that each member of the panel is aware of this running order. It is important to adhere to this, so appoint a strong chairperson to regulate the proceedings strictly.

When organizing a group presentation, research the background of your chosen speakers carefully – it is vital to have the right balance among the participants. If they are too like-minded, there will be little discussion generated by their speeches; if their ideas clash, they may react to one another with hostility while on the podium. If necessary, build in time for a final question-and-answer session between the panel and audience.

THINGS TO DO

1. Book a venue with the facilities to cope with group presentations.
2. Check that there are no personal animosities between proposed speakers.
3. Invite the speakers, and confirm their attendance.
4. Discuss the running order of the speeches.
5. Draw up a rigid timetable.
6. Appoint a strong individual to act as chairperson.

12 Research your audience before sending invitations to a presentation.

INVITING AN AUDIENCE

When thinking about who should attend a presentation, bear in mind the following points:
● Who would benefit from hearing the information in the presentation?
● What would you like the audience to learn from the presentation?
● How can you reach the target audience?
Planning your publicity is an integral part of the organizational process. Once you have decided on your target audience, ensure that advertising is placed where they will see it – for example, in an appropriate trade publication. The time, date, and venue should be clearly visible. Have personal invitations sent to anyone you wish to attend.

KNOWING YOUR VENUE

If possible, visit your chosen presentation venue in advance to check out the layout. If this is not practical, ask the organizers to send you a detailed floorplan showing all the facilities. Consider the lighting, acoustics, seating, and power supply carefully.

13 Assess all details of a venue, no matter how minor they may appear.

ASSESSING THE VENUE

The venue will set the mood of your presentation. An informal gathering in a sunny room on a university campus will put an audience in a very different frame of mind than will the sterile conference hall of a large hotel. If you visit the venue in advance, note down as many details as possible – including its atmosphere and size. Assess your venue at the same time of day as your presentation will be given so that you will be able to make informed decisions about the seating and lighting. Take the opportunity to check out the locations of doorways, power points, light switches, and refreshment facilities.

Keep area around doorway clear for easy entry and exit

Position refreshments at the rear of the venue to avoid possible distractions

Locate power points, and check whether you need extension leads

Lower window blinds to shut out light when projecting visual aids on to screen

14 Locate the light switches so that, if necessary, you can dim the lights to use your visual aids.

▲ ASSESSING THE BASICS
When visiting a venue in advance, try to assess whether there are any awkward obstructions that might hide you from the audience. Check the positions of doorways, power points, and other facilities, and get a feel for the atmosphere of the room.

15 Decide on the positioning of any visual aids well in advance.

CONSIDERING THE DETAILS

When assessing a venue, take careful stock of its location – is it accessible to your audience? Is it near an airport, railway station, or underground? Is the venue on the flight path of a major airport, or next to a noisy restaurant? Are there immovable features that could restrict the audience's view? If so, plan your seating around these. Can you control the heating or air conditioning? If so, adjust the temperature to just below what is comfortable, since considerable warmth will be generated by a large number of people being together in one room.

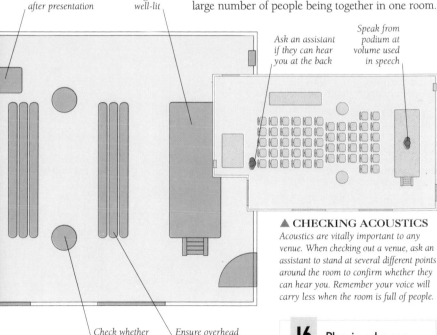

Provide a place for audience to collect handouts after presentation

Make sure stage is well-lit

Ask an assistant if they can hear you at the back

Speak from podium at volume used in speech

Check whether column restricts audience view

Ensure overhead lighting is as natural as possible

▲ CHECKING ACOUSTICS

Acoustics are vitally important to any venue. When checking out a venue, ask an assistant to stand at several different points around the room to confirm whether they can hear you. Remember your voice will carry less when the room is full of people.

16 Plan in advance how you will make your exit.

SEATING THE AUDIENCE

It is important to get the right balance when seating your audience. Comfort is an obvious factor to consider, but you must ensure that your audience is not so comfortable that they fall asleep, or so uncomfortable that they start fidgeting before you reach the end of your presentation. Ideally, chairs should be upright and of equal size. If you can adjust the seating, place chairs far enough apart to allow people to put their bags and briefcases on the floor beside them. Spacing the chairs out in this way will also prevent the audience from feeling claustrophobic. If you think your audience will want to take notes during your presentation, provide chairs with armrests on which to balance notepads. To ensure that the seats in the front of the auditorium fill up first, remove seats from the rear. Keep a number of accessible spare seats in reserve to put out for any latecomers. Finally, be sure to comply with the venue's fire safety regulations with regard to seating arrangements.

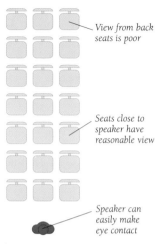

View from back seats is poor

Seats close to speaker have reasonable view

Speaker can easily make eye contact

▲ **PLAN ONE**
A series of straight, narrow rows allows the speaker to make eye contact with all of the audience. However, this layout does not provide a good view or acoustics for people seated at the back of the venue.

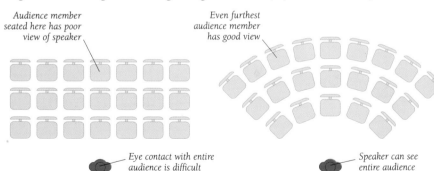

Audience member seated here has poor view of speaker

Even furthest audience member has good view

Eye contact with entire audience is difficult

Speaker can see entire audience

▲ **PLAN TWO**
Here an audience of the same size as that in Plan One is seated closer to the speaker. The majority of the audience has a good view of the speaker and is near enough to hear the presentation clearly. The speaker has to work hard to make eye contact with everyone.

▲ **PLAN THREE**
This semi-circular layout is popular as it provides the optimum arrangement for acoustics and visibility – but the disadvantage is that it takes up more space than Plans One and Two. The speaker can maintain strong eye contact with all members of the audience.

CHECKING THE VENUE'S AUDIO-VISUAL FACILITIES

If you intend to use audio-visual elements in your presentation, you must check that the appropriate facilities are available at the venue, and that they function correctly. Familiarize yourself with each piece of equipment to avoid any delays or mistakes during the presentation. Large venues will require the use of a basic public address system (PA) comprising speakers, an amplifier, and one or more microphones. If a PA is not available, you will have to bring and install your own – they can be hired. Make sure is it powerful enough for the venue room. Ensure that there is a screen on which to project any images, checking that the size of the screen is appropriate to the size of the venue, and that it is in view of the whole audience.

17 Ensure that you know how the public address system functions.

18 Keep spare seats in reserve for any latecomers.

USING A MICROPHONE

A microphone is needed only when you are speaking to a large audience, or if you are speaking in the open air. If you need to use one, always test it in advance, making adjustments for volume and background noise. Hand-held or podium microphones tend to restrict movement, so if you will need to demonstrate visual aids use a wireless hand-held model. Clip-on microphones allow you to use both hands while presenting your speech, but always be sure to position them correctly otherwise they can exaggerate noises such as breathing or turning pages.

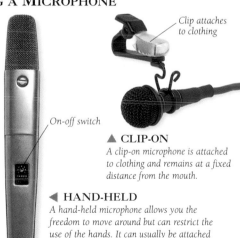

Clip attaches to clothing

On-off switch

▲ **CLIP-ON**
A clip-on microphone is attached to clothing and remains at a fixed distance from the mouth.

◀ **HAND-HELD**
A hand-held microphone allows you the freedom to move around but can restrict the use of the hands. It can usually be attached to a podium, adding to its versatility.

CLARIFYING OBJECTIVES

Before you prepare for a presentation, it is important that you think about your objectives. Do you want to entertain the audience, pass on vital information, or inspire them to rush off and take immediate action as a consequence of your speech?

19 Structure your speech around three or four main points.

SETTING THE TONE

The general tone and style of your presentation can reinforce the purpose of your speech. If you want to pass on information, then you need to take a logically consistent, well-structured approach to your subject matter. If your main purpose is to entertain, include some jokes, anecdotes, and funny stories. If you want to inspire the audience, keep the content of your speech positive and pitched at a level at which they can respond personally and emotionally.

20 Keep the audience interested by including a few relevant anecdotes.

ENCOURAGING RESPONSES

Every speaker wants to give a successful and well-received presentation, but many do not know that there are practical methods to achieve this. By structuring your speech in certain ways, you can elicit the response you want from the audience. For example, if you are providing your audience with new information, you may want them to ask questions at the end of your speech. Whet their appetites for the subject by not telling them everything they need to know immediately, but encouraging them to be inquisitive.

▼ USING THE THREE ES
Each successful presentation has three essential objectives. The first aim is to educate: the audience should learn something from your speech. The second is to entertain: the audience should enjoy your speech. The final element is to explain: all parts of your speech should be clear to your audience.

Educate ➤ **Entertain** ➤ **Explain**

USING YOUR KNOWLEDGE

The main objective of making a presentation is to relay information to your audience and nothing is more likely to capture and hold their attention than your enthusiasm for the subject. Do not get too carried away with your preparation – plan to lead your audience with your enthusiasm rather than overwhelm them with it. Authoritative knowledge usually speaks for itself, so there is no need for you to drop names or academic references if you really know your subject. You will gain credibility if you handle audience questions adeptly, so be well-informed and well-prepared.

21 Make sure you deliver the main concepts of your presentation clearly.

22 Summarize your main points in one sentence.

SELECTING KEY POINTS

Every adult audience has a limited attention span of about 45 minutes. In that time, they will absorb only about a third of what was said, and a maximum of seven concepts. Limit yourself to three or four main points, and emphasize them at the beginning of your speech, in the middle, and again at the end to reiterate your message. Try to find a catchy title that sums up your speech, but avoid being too clever or too obscure. "The Role of TQM in BPR" is fine for managers in your company who know that you are intending to talk about the concepts of total quality management and business process re-engineering, but it is no use making your title so cryptic that you confuse even the most informed audiences. Your audience will be most open to you if they have a clear idea of the subject of your speech.

FIRST THOUGHTS

Lorem ipsum dolor sit amet, consectetuer adipiscing elit, sed diam nonummy nibh euismod tincidunt ut laoreet dolore magna aliquam erat volutpat. Ut wisi enim ad minim veniam, quis nostrud exerci tation ullamcorper suscipit lobortis nisl ut aliquip ex ea commodo consequat.

Ut wisi enim ad minim veniam, quis nostrud exerci tation ullamcorper suscipit lobortis nisl ut aliquip ex ea commodo consequat. Duis autem vel eum iriure dolor in hendrerit in vulputate velit esse molestie consequat, vel illum dolore eu feugiat nulla facilisis at vero eros et accumsan et iusto odio dignissim qui blandit praesent luptatum zzril

Nam liber tempor cum soluta nobis eleifend option congue ni impediet doming id quod mazi placerat facer possim ass. Lorem ipsum dolor sit amet, consect adipiselit, sed diam nonummy nibh euismod tincidunt ut laor dolore magna aliquam erat ex eavolupat. Ut wisi enim ad mi veniam, quis nostrud exercition ullamcorper suse lobortis nisl ut aliquip ex ea commodo conse. Duis autem vel eum iriure dolor in hendrerit in vulputate velit esse molestie consequat, v in hendrerit in vulputate velit esse

Key Points

A. Why the training course is necessary.

B. What the training will involve.

C. What the end results of the training are hoped to be, and what the benefits are.

▲ CHOOSING YOUR MAIN POINTS

Clarify your ideas by summarizing the main ideas from your notes into succinct points. Limit yourself to three or four points to keep your message simple and memorable.

FINDING MATERIAL

A successful presentation always begins with careful background research. This requires initiative and hard work, and can be time-consuming. Allocate sufficient time for your research, and explore as many sources as possible, from press cuttings to the Internet.

23 Keep your main objectives in mind while researching your material.

A. Why the training course is necessary.

B. What the training will involve.

C. What the end results of the training are hoped to be, and what the benefits are.

▲ USING YOUR MAIN POINTS

When you begin your research, keep the three or four main points in mind. As you find material relevant to your speech, organize it into separate files for each main point until you have enough to fill out your presentation.

FINDING SOURCES

A good starting point for research is to review one of the leading books on the subject of your presentation, and to look at its bibliography. From there you should be able to find a large amount of relevant reference material. For newspaper or magazine articles, consider using a press-cuttings agency, which, for a fee, will supply you regularly with a package of articles on virtually any subject that you care to name. This will provide you with the free time to explore the many other sources of information available, for example:

- Management reports, government papers, and professional journals;
- Friends, family, and other personal contacts;
- Videos, CD-ROMs, and the Internet.

RESEARCHING MATERIAL

At the beginning of your research, allow yourself enough time to consider thoroughly the advantages and disadvantages of every source of information you intend to use. Be realistic about what you hope to find out from each source, and think about how best to use the information in your speech. Always consult your personal contacts for any leads; there is nothing more frustrating than spending days in a library only to find that a friend of a friend is the greatest living expert on your subject.

24 Try different sources to see which you find the most helpful.

FRESHENING UP YOUR RESEARCH

Be open-minded when starting on your research, and seek out fresh fields of research to enliven your presentation. Do not rely on dusty old books – explore new reference sources on the Internet to glean the latest information on your subject. Your speech will be all the more appealing to the audience if it sounds innovative rather than like a rehash of old information from oft-quoted sources. Make the audience feel that you are feeding them new knowledge by providing fresh information around your basic facts and figures.

▲ MAKING GOOD USE OF YOUR TIME
It is important to decide very quickly whether or not a particular avenue of research is worth pursuing. Once you begin to find relevant information, note its source and its main points. Is it the most up-to-date material on the subject? Is the information accurate? Is it giving you any new leads or areas of research? Persevere only with the material that fills your research criteria.

▲ EXPLORING WEB SITES
Each Web site on the Internet holds a wealth of information that can be accessed, saved, or printed out, and used as reference material. One of the chief advantages of this mode of research is that the information Web sites hold is usually more frequently updated than the same information in print.

USING NEW TECHNOLOGY

The Internet brings an international electronic library right on to your desk. Use well-chosen key words to search for relevant reference material from the extraordinary range of information available on the Internet – new sites are springing up daily. The more specific your key words are, the more chance you have of finding the data you require within a reasonable length of time. Store large amounts of material on computerized data bases, which can be purchased as ready-made software packages or designed specifically for your purposes.

25 Do not ignore a good source just because the information is not immediately accessible to you.

21

STRUCTURING MATERIAL

The order in which you present the main points of your presentation, and the emphasis each point is given, will affect the message that your audience takes away. Use the most appropriate structure in your speech to give your audience the right message.

26 Decide how many points you intend to make in your presentation.

CHOOSING A STRUCTURE

There are several ways in which you can present your three or four main points. You may choose to introduce them separately, either one after the other in order of importance, or chronologically, or in any other sequence that makes sense. If you want one particular point to give the strongest impression, present it first, and follow it with supporting points – or any other points that you are making. Alternatively, interweave your points to highlight their equal significance. The structure most commonly used by speakers is to overlap the main points that are being made. This way, an idea can be left open and referred back to in response to subsequent ideas in the presentation.

27 Make sure that your presentation ends on a strong, positive point.

▲ MAKING SEPARATE POINTS
Here ideas that do not necessarily flow into each other can be presented separately and given equal weight. Remember, an audience may assume that the first point has greater significance.

▲ OVERLAPPING POINTS
In practice, the most frequently occurring structure is the one in which each point overlaps and depends to some extent upon the others. The second point has to be partially unveiled in order to explain the first, and so on. Each subsequent point can be referred to in relation to the earlier points, linking all the main points together.

▲ EMPHASIZING ONE POINT
If one point is of greater significance than the others, put it first and allow it the most time so that you can discuss it fully. Back it up or complement it with your secondary or supporting points.

MATCHING PRESENTATION STRUCTURE TO MATERIAL

TYPES OF STRUCTURE	PRACTICAL USES
MAKING SEPARATE POINTS Points are presented in a sequence that suits the particular subject.	Formal presentations, such as a serious educational talk or a lecture on management theory, can benefit from this presentation structure. If the audience members are taking notes, the speaker can assist them by summarizing each point after it has been made and providing a brief introduction to lead into the following point.
EMPHASIZING ONE POINT The main point is followed by several other points.	Examples of this type of presentation might include a talk given to staff about the need for improved customer service. The structure is emphatic and is suitable for use when the audience is well-informed about the subject matter and can grasp a high level of detail. It is also useful if you want to present another aspect of the same subject.
OVERLAPPING POINTS Points are referred back to or reintroduced for emphasis.	This structure is most suitable for informal talks given in front of a small audience. It is often used in meetings attended by close colleagues, who are familiar with the subject matter and can cope with a relatively complex presentation. Overlapping points encourage debate and audience intervention as different ideas present themselves.

USING NARRATIVE

The basic technique of narrative is to give your subject a recognizable beginning, middle, and end. The most common use of this technique is in storytelling. For your presentation to be a success, it is important that you follow this basic format when composing your speech. The introduction to your presentation is the beginning; the middle section consists of your central themes and ideas (using whichever structure you decide best suits your purpose); while the end is formed by your conclusion, referring back to your main themes, and then taking questions from the audience if necessary. Remember that it is important to give the audience clear signposts at the beginning and end of each stage of your presentation.

▲ USING SYMBOLS
Think laterally when structuring your speech. Choose familiar images to support your ideas, such as a cat to show instinctive behaviour. Look outside your original field of research for analogies that illustrate points vividly.

USING AN OUTLINE

It is helpful to prepare a written outline of the material that you wish to present. This will help to clarify the structure of your presentation while you are writing it and can be used to jog your memory while you are making the presentation. Think of your three or four main points as A, B, C, and D, and then put subheadings under each one (1, 2, 3). Label any secondary subheadings as i), ii), iii), and so on. When writing these notes, keep them simple so that they are easy to read at a glance.

A. Why training is needed.
   1. Staff benefit from refresher course.
   2. New staff will learn correct procedures.

Main points are labelled alphabetically

B. What training involves.
   1. Improving performance.
     i) Tests of skill level.
     ii) Gaps in knowledge.
   2. Practicalities.

Subheadings are labelled with Arabic numerals

C. Expected end results.
   1. Improved efficiency.
   2. Greater productivity.

Secondary subheadings are labelled with Roman numerals

▲ **OUTLINING A STRUCTURE**
Make up a rough outline of the structure you are planning for your presentation, as in the sample above. Use this as a basis from which to expand on your theme while you are researching and preparing your presentation.

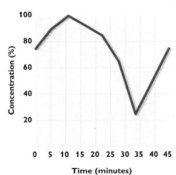

▲ **AUDIENCE ATTENTION SPAN**
This chart shows a typical audience's attention span, based on a 45-minute presentation. Audiences are most alert just after the start of a presentation, reaching a peak at about 10 minutes. Attention fades until 30–35 minutes have passed, then increases as the presentation nears its end.

OPENING EFFECTIVELY

It is essential to make a good impression at the beginning of your presentation, and one of the best ways to do this is for you to appear positive and confident. This means you must first be well-prepared. Seasoned presenters who prefer not to use notes invariably write out their first sentence or two. That way, they can concentrate more on the impression they are giving, and less on the words they are speaking. Plan an effective opening that provides the audience with an outline of the presentation you are about to give, informing them briefly of the points you will be making during your speech. Use anecdotes to break the ice and draw the audience into your speech in a familiar way. Always remember, however, that the audience is not at its most alert at the very beginning of your speech, so save your strongest point for a few minutes into the presentation.

LINKING AND SUMMING UP

It is important to incorporate clear signposts into your presentation. Plan a logical flow of ideas and themes to help the audience follow your presentation easily, and introduce new subjects by making clear links between the old and new ideas. Listen to professional speakers on radio and television, and note the techniques they use to link together the points or themes of their speeches and sum up each point before introducing a new one. These links and summaries are as important as the main points themselves, so plan them well.

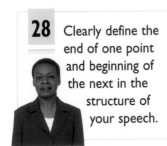

28 Clearly define the end of one point and beginning of the next in the structure of your speech.

USING REPETITION

Recapping information during your presentation is an effective way of reinforcing the main points of your argument. When structuring your speech, build some repetition into its framework at the end of each main point and in the conclusion. However, simply repeating the information you have already delivered in the main body of your speech is not enough. Use different wording to keep the ideas sounding fresh, yet familiar.

29 Do not change the tone of your voice too often; this can sound false.

ENDING MEMORABLY

Structuring a strong ending to your presentation is as important as planning a good beginning – it is vital to signal to your audience that the end of your speech is approaching. Insert phrases such as "for my final point..." or "in conclusion..." to alert the audience to the fact that you are about to summarize all that you have said. They will be grateful for the opportunity to catch up on any points they may have missed during your speech.

▼ REINFORCING POINTS

It is important to reinforce the main points of any presentation. You can do this by first giving the audience a "contents list" of your speech, then discussing the issues you are raising, and finishing off with a summary.

Tell them what you are going to tell them → Tell them → Tell them what you have told them

WRITING A PRESENTATION

It is important to be aware that written material can sound very different when it is delivered to an audience in spoken form. Learn to write your prose in a natural oral style that follows natural speech patterns and is suitable for verbal presentation.

30 Remember that writing a speech is different from hearing it read.

STARTING TO WRITE

Once you have completed all your research and outlined the structure of your presentation, you are ready to start writing. Try to imagine your words as you would like your audience to hear them. Spend some quiet time alone thinking about what you will write, then compose a first draft by writing down – without stopping – everything that you think you would like to include. If you are unsure about how to write for speech, prepare by assessing the difference between spoken and written language.

31 Find different ways for expressing the same idea. Use the most natural one.

ADAPTING WRITING STYLES FOR SPEECH

SENTENCE STRUCTURE	SPEAKING RATHER THAN WRITING
GRAMMAR Try to avoid sentences that are grammatically correct but sound stilted when spoken. To sound direct, use the first and second person (*I* and *you*) and active verbs.	*Say*: "The accounting system I work with", *not* "The accounting system with which I work".
	Say: "You must recognize these ploys for what they are", *not* "It is important that these ploys are recognized...".
SYNTAX Always put the most important or interesting facts first. Do not begin a sentence with a subordinate clause or with any statement that could be put in parentheses.	*Say*: "Lower costs and increased output – that's what we need", *not* "We need to reduce costs and increase output".
	Say: "This can make all the difference", *not* "Although this may seem a minor detail, it can make all the difference...".

STREAMLINING MATERIAL

Once you have produced the first draft of your presentation, you can begin to hone down the material. Read through your draft to ensure that you have prioritized the facts correctly and included all the essential information. Fill in your material with relevant examples to reinforce your main points. Finally, use items of particular interest or appeal, which are not essential but will enhance audience enjoyment of your presentation, to add humour and topicality to your speech.

32 Be particular about what you include in the presentation.

▼ PRIORITIZING LEVELS OF INFORMATION
Before you begin, write down every point relevant to the theme of your presentation, and put each in one of these categories.

Must know ➤ **Should know** ➤ **Nice to know**

WRITING TO SOUND NATURAL

The best starting point for giving a successful presentation is that you feel confident and relaxed about the words you are delivering, so when you are writing your speech, keep your sentence construction simple. Think about your audience as a single person – this will help to create an atmosphere of intimacy. Speakers who succeed in doing this make every member of the audience feel that their message is directed uniquely at them, which holds their attention. If you are not sure whether you sound natural, tape-record yourself reading a draft of your speech, then listen and amend your text where necessary.

DO'S AND DON'TS

✔ Do use simple, direct sentences.	✘ Don't use jargon or inappropriate language.
✔ Do use the pronouns "you" and "I".	✘ Don't fill your speech with irrelevant points.
✔ Do use active verbs (run, go, do, use, etc.).	✘ Don't feel that you have to write out the speech word for word.
✔ Do sprinkle your speech liberally with adjectives.	✘ Don't overwhelm the audience with too much detail.
✔ Do prepare and rehearse phrases to avoid stumbling.	✘ Don't patronize your audience.
✔ Do include examples and analogies to illustrate your points.	✘ Don't try to imitate someone else's style; it will sound false.

33 Make sure the written structure of your presentation is not too complex, or it may be confusing.

CONDENSING A PRESENTATION INTO NOTES

If you choose to deliver a presentation using notes, begin by writing a full draft of the presentation, including all your main points and the examples you will use to illustrate and explain them. This script is the starting point from which you can begin to condense your prose into notes. Using clearly numbered note cards, pick out the key words and phrases from your script, and write them legibly on one side of card. Do not write too much on each card, and keep the information simple and unambiguous.

◄ PREPARING A DRAFT
Having decided on the structure of your presentation and then compiled your research material, write (or type) the speech out in full. Edit and re-edit this draft until you are satisfied with the flow and pace of the speech.

◄ PREPARING NOTES
Extract the major points from the final draft, and write them on numbered cards. Limit your notes to two points per card for clarity.

PACING A SPEECH

Think about what makes a good speech work well. More often than not, it is the timing. The silent parts of a speech – in other words, the pauses – are just as important as the spoken words in communicating the content of the speech, since they provide aural punctuation. When writing your speech, consider how it will sound to your audience. Whether you choose to read the presentation from notes or as a full script, write "pause" wherever you feel a break is necessary – for example, where a point requires emphasis, or to mark a break between one clear idea and another. Include these pauses when rehearsing. Using silence takes courage: a scripted pause should last about three seconds – much longer than a pause in your normal speech.

34 Print your speech on one side of the page only, and use a large typeface.

35 Always number the pages of a full, written speech.

PREPARING NOTE CARDS

Regard using notes during a presentation as an insurance against forgetting your speech – you do not have to read from them parrot-fashion, but you have the security of knowing that they are there if your mind goes blank. Notes are meant to provide a series of cues to remind you what you want to say, and in what order, allowing you to talk to the audience instead of reciting your presentation to them. There are a number of useful techniques you can use if speaking from notes, such as condensing a preprepared outline, writing key sentences, or noting key words – but write out quotations and jokes in full unless you are sure you know them. Use a system of colour coding to mark text that you can cut from your speech without compromising the integrity of your message if, for instance, you run over your allotted time. For example, write essential text in blue ink, and write text that can be cut in green ink.

36 Make notes on firm paper or index cards.

▲ USING PROMPTS
Transfer key words and phrases from your presentation on to cards. Be straightforward in what you write down so that you are able to remember the point of each prompt.

PREPARING A WRITTEN SCRIPT

If you choose to use a written script in your presentation, it is essential to arrange it carefully. Use large type and double line-spacing so that the text is easy to read. Set out the headings clearly so that it is easy to keep your place. Use a variety of different styling methods, such as emboldening or italicizing, to highlight the text that you want to emphasize. Finally, print the finished document on to sturdy paper, and keep a spare copy.

Gap in text marks break between subjects

Large, clear typeface is used

Key phrases are highlighted for emphasis

TRAINING
Good afternoon.
My name is John Smith and I am from the company's
Training Department.

What I am going to talk to you about today is Training. (PAUSE)
More specifically, I'm going to be talking about three points:
Why training is necessary;
What the training involves; and
What the expected end results are.

1

Title heads first page of script

Pauses are marked

Each page is numbered

▲ LAYING OUT A WRITTEN SCRIPT
Highlight emphases and pauses when laying out your script – this will help you to speak naturally and confidently to your audience, which is essential for a smooth-running presentation.

USING AUDIO-VISUAL AIDS

Audio-visual (AV) aids can be central to a presentation, as they are often able to illustrate difficult concepts more easily than words. Always ask yourself if using AV aids will contribute to your presentation, and never be tempted to use them unnecessarily.

37 Always rehearse your presentation using your chosen audio-visual aids.

USING DIFFERENT AUDIO-VISUAL AIDS

TYPES OF AUDIO-VISUAL AID

EXAMPLES OF AUDIO-VISUAL AID

LOW COMPLEXITY
The advantage of these aids is their simplicity, and in the fact that no power supply is needed for them to work. Information can be prepared in advance, leaving little to set up on the day. Handouts can be prepared for any size of audience, but boards and flip-charts need to be visible and are best for small audiences.

HANDOUTS
Distribute these before giving your presentation, preferably during a break. Make sure that you give the handouts a purpose by referring to them during your presentation.

MEDIUM COMPLEXITY
This group contains some of the most commonly used AV aids, which achieve good effects without involving too much technical hardware. The aids themselves need setting up on the day of your presentation, but the information and any slides used in conjunction with them can be prepared in advance.

SLIDE PROJECTOR
Arrange the slides you need to illustrate your arguments in a carousel prior to your speech. Practise operating the projector before you give your presentation.

HIGH COMPLEXITY
These aids involve the very highest level of technical capability and may require a specialized team to set them up. The impact achieved using high-complexity AV aids can be stunning and well worth the work, but there is more opportunity for breakdown or failure the more complex the AV aid.

VIDEO
Use video to show short live-action images or a taped message from a speaker who is not able to attend the presentation in person.

CHOOSING AV AIDS

There is a range of AV aids to suit different types of presentation. Such aids can sometimes distance you from the audience, however, so use them only if they are appropriate and helpful. AV aids have varying levels of complexity; many require a source of electricity, which can lead to problems if the power fails; others may need to be designed or installed by specialists and may be difficult to use.

38 Pause when you first ask your audience to look at a visual aid.

WRITING BOARD
Use a writing board to illustrate your points in an informal presentation to a small audience. Make sure that your writing is legible to the people sitting at the back of the audience.

FLIP-CHART
Prepare any number of sheets in advance, using charts and diagrams to highlight your arguments. Emphasize key points with colour, and ensure that the flip-chart can be seen by everyone in the audience.

OVERHEAD PROJECTOR
This is the best way of presenting charts and tables. Use a pointer to draw attention to particular graphs or numbers without obscuring the audience's view of the image.

AUDIO SYSTEM
An audio system with headphones is vital if you have to provide simultaneous translation facilities. A microphone, amplifier, and speakers are also handy for large audiences.

MULTIMEDIA
Use CD-ROM packages with moving images and an audio track on a large monitor with speakers. Alternatively, employ a software engineer to create a package to your specific requirements.

COMPUTER GRAPHICS
Software can be used to display graphs, charts, or three-dimensional images on screen. Moving graphics can be used to show how statistics will change over time.

CONSIDERING AUDIENCE SIZE

Different AV aids suit different sizes of audience, but if your resources are limited you can adapt your AV aids to suit any audience. For example, if you are using computer graphics but want to avoid losing definition of images by enlarging them too much, provide each member of the audience with handouts of the computer graphics you are showing on-screen. Alternatively, if you are presenting to a large audience, project the images on to several large screens.

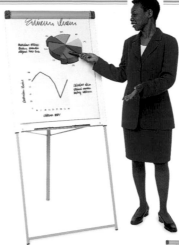

◀ **VIEW FROM A SMALL AUDIENCE**
When presenting to a small audience sitting close to you, your visual aids will be clearly visible to everyone – whichever type you choose to use.

39 Number your slides to avoid any confusion.

VIEW FROM A ▶ LARGE AUDIENCE
Visual aids that work for a small audience are unlikely to work for a large one. An audience sitting far away may be unable to discern much from them.

PREPARING AV AIDS

All AV aids require considerable preparation, but whereas a writing board can be set up relatively quickly and then used over again, a multimedia demonstration can take a long time to prepare. Generally speaking, the higher the complexity of the AV aid, the more preparation is required.

If you do not have the time, the knowledge, or the creative talent to prepare your own AV aids, enlist somebody to do it for you. Use support staff, a colleague, or an external design agency. Choose your helper carefully, and present them with a tight brief to prevent any misinterpretation regarding the desired final product.

POINTS TO REMEMBER

● Audiences read on-screen material faster than you can speak it, so do not read it out loud for their benefit.

● While one half of the audience will be looking at your visual material, the other half will be looking at you. Stand still when you want the audience to concentrate on visual material.

● If you plan to re-use your AV aids, make sure you arrange to have them collected after your presentation.

MAKING AN IMPACT

During your preparation time, you may find that you can make information easier to understand and express abstract ideas more clearly by adding design elements to visual aids. Keep all visual aids simple and uncluttered, and use design elements consistently. Use bold colours – subtleties between pastels do not carry across a crowded room. The sections on a pie diagram can be completely lost if the colours used are not sufficiently contrasting.

When using video, show long segments that illustrate and complement your points, rather than short bursts, which can distract the audience's attention from the essence of your speech.

40 Use cartoons to make serious points lighter.

41 Write notes on the frames of overhead projector slides.

ASSEMBLING TOOLS

Think carefully about which items you may need in order to make proper use of your chosen AV aids. For example:

● A laser pointer to indicate items on screens, writing boards, or flip-charts;

● Two sets of chalk or special marker pens to use on writing boards;

● Blank acetate sheets for use with an overhead projector;

● Spare flip-chart;

● Extension lead;

● Back-up disks and spare cable for multimedia presentations;

● Copies of videos or slides;

● Adapters, if taking electrical equipment abroad.

KNOWING YOUR AV AIDS

By the time you actually come to give your presentation, you should be fully aware of how to operate any high-complexity AV aids you have chosen to augment your subject matter. Even if you do not enjoy working with multimedia or video aids, there are instances in which the effort (and the additional expense of creating them) is worthwhile, even for a small audience.

On rare occasions when using high-complexity AV aids, you may be unlucky enough to experience technical problems. If you do not have the requisite expertise to deal with these hitches, ensure that someone who does will be present at the venue to help you out. Always take along a series of low-complexity aids, such as handouts, as a back-up, or be prepared to go without any AV aids at all.

42 Take duplicates of all audio-visual materials that you know you cannot do without in your speech.

REHEARSING

Rehearsal is a vital part of preparing for a successful presentation. It is an ideal opportunity to memorize and time your material and to smooth over any rough edges in your delivery. Practise with your AV aids, and allow time for questions at the end.

43 Practise losing your place in your script or notes – and finding it again.

POINTS TO REMEMBER

● You cannot rehearse too much. If you are confident with your material, your audience will have confidence in you.

● The time you will have to speak includes time you will spend using AV aids and answering questions from the audience, so allow for this when rehearsing.

● Rehearsals should rely less and less on the script each time.

● Sample questions should be prepared beforehand, so you can practise answering them and estimate timing.

PRACTISING ALOUD

The main point of a rehearsal is to memorize your material and the order in which you are going to present it. This is your best opportunity to fine-tune the content of your speech, and to ensure that all your points are delivered with the weight and significance you intend. Start rehearsals by simply reading through your full script. Once you are comfortable with the material, begin to practise in front of the mirror, and switch to notes if you are using them. The first attempt may make you feel slightly nervous and uncomfortable, but your confidence should build with each rehearsal, so that you are well-prepared when you stand before your real audience and begin your presentation.

DEVELOPING SPONTANEITY

Only when you are freed from slavish reliance on your script or notes can you begin to feel and sound spontaneous. Speaking off the cuff to an audience is a very different discipline to presenting a rehearsed speech. However, it need not be such a daunting task. Develop the trick of apparent "spontaneity" by knowing your subject inside out. In doing this, you give yourself confidence to add details or examples that have not been written into your speech, thus making your presentation sound fresh, off-the-cuff, and unrehearsed.

44 Practise speaking clearly both in normal tones and at volume.

INVITING FEEDBACK

When you feel ready, begin to practise your speech aloud in front of a friend or colleague, and ask for honest and constructive criticism. Invite your "audience" to point out areas where they feel improvements could be made and to suggest how you can make them. Your audience should bear in mind the context in which the presentation is going to be made, so explain it to them clearly. Try to reproduce the conditions of the presentation, especially the distance between you and the front row of your audience, as closely as possible. That way you can get a sense of how well your voice will carry. Learn to control your voice so that it will sound the same to the audience whether you are presenting in an auditorium or to a small group in a meeting room.

45 Vary the pace of your speech, and decide which pace is most effective.

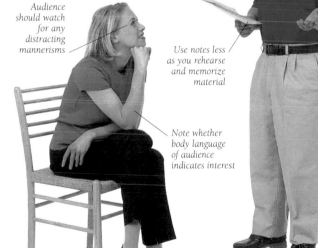

Audience should watch for any distracting mannerisms

Use notes less as you rehearse and memorize material

Note whether body language of audience indicates interest

Use hand gestures that reinforce your message

◀ **PRACTISING WITH AN AUDIENCE**
Rehearsing in front of a friend will build your confidence. Ask their opinion of both your vocal and physical delivery; enjoy their praise, but acknowledge any criticisms or advice for improvement that they might suggest.

PREPARING YOURSELF

It is as important to prepare yourself as it is to prepare your speech. The overall impact of your presentation will be determined as much by how you appear as by what you say.

BELIEVING IN YOURSELF

A positive self-image is all-important for delivering a successful presentation. Identify your strengths, and make the most of them. Except in very rare cases, the audience is as keen as you are for your presentation to be interesting and successful.

 46 An audience is your ally. Its members want to learn from you.

THINKING POSITIVELY

Repeat positive and encouraging thoughts to yourself as you prepare for your presentation and just before it to help boost your confidence and allay any last-minute fears and nerves. For example, try some of the following phrases:

❝ My presentation is interesting and full of great ideas. The audience will love it. ❞

❝ The audience is sure to be enthusiastic. My presentation is strong, and I'm well prepared. ❞

❝ I know my subject inside out. The audience will discover that for themselves early on. ❞

❝ My rehearsals went really well. I can't wait to see the reaction of the audience. ❞

VISUALIZING SUCCESS

When preparing for a presentation, train yourself to visualize the scenario positively. Picture an enthusiastic audience loving your successful presentation. You have a message to convey to the audience, and you are being given the perfect opportunity to do so. Imagine your audience taking notes, laughing at any jokes or anecdotes that you may use, and asking interesting and constructive questions at the end. Visualize the body language of the audience's positive response, and imagine yourself making eye contact with members of the audience to encourage the positive rapport developing between you.

 47 Behave naturally, and an audience will warm to you.

48 Think of a large audience as if it were a small group.

▼ PICTURING PERFECTION
Increase your confidence by imagining yourself giving a perfect presentation. Visualize the enthusiastic, interested faces of the audience listening to your speech.

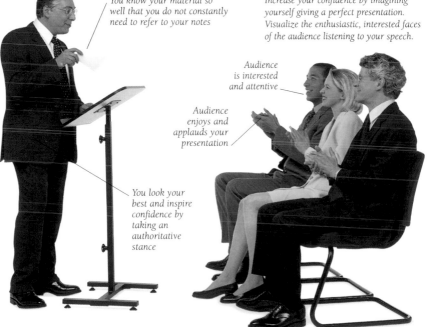

You know your material so well that you do not constantly need to refer to your notes

Audience is interested and attentive

Audience enjoys and applauds your presentation

You look your best and inspire confidence by taking an authoritative stance

ANALYZING APPEARANCE

Your audience will be greatly affected by the way you look, but it is not always easy to judge your own appearance and the impression you are creating. Ask friends or colleagues to comment on your image and help you to adjust it to suit your audience.

49 Study yourself in a mirror to see what impression you make.

POINTS TO REMEMBER

● A good night's sleep is essential before the day of your presentation.

● A hair brush, toothbrush, travel iron, clothes brush, and shoe buffer are useful items to take to the venue, so that you can look your best for your presentation.

● Zips and buttons should be fastened, and your shirt should be tucked in before you enter the presentation room.

● A jacket can be worn to hide any marks that may appear, if perspiration is a problem.

MAKING AN IMPRESSION

First impressions are strong, and very hard to change. Think about how quickly you make judgments about people you meet for the first time. Signals can be picked up very quickly from the way people dress, the way they walk, and even from the way they stand. Before you reach the lectern, your audience will have formed an opinion of you based on these first impressions. It is important to decide on the image you want to convey to your audience early on. Making the right first impression may be vital to the success of your presentation, so dress appropriately, and walk, speak, and stand with confidence, to achieve the right first impression.

KNOWING THE AUDIENCE

Your message will be best received if the audience can identify with you, so it is important always to be aware of the audience's perception of the image you present. If you know a little about your audience, it is easier to decide on the impression that you want to create. Remember, particular styles of dress can communicate specific messages to each different audience. For example, consider how a factory manager will be perceived who addresses the shopfloor workforce wearing a suit in comparison to one dressed in overalls.

50 Do not wear anything that may distract the audience.

AVOIDING PITFALLS

Check the clothes that you are going to wear in advance to prevent the problem of having to wear ill-fitting or unlaundered clothes at your presentation. If you want to look your absolute best for the presentation, bring the outfit with you, and change into it before you begin your last-minute preparation. Check that changing facilities are available at the venue before you arrive.

51 Keep your hands out of your pockets during the presentation.

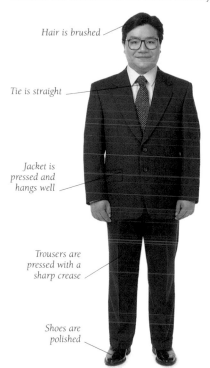

Hair is brushed

Tie is straight

Jacket is pressed and hangs well

Trousers are pressed with a sharp crease

Shoes are polished

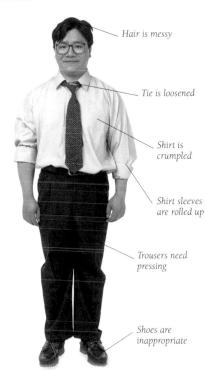

Hair is messy

Tie is loosened

Shirt is crumpled

Shirt sleeves are rolled up

Trousers need pressing

Shoes are inappropriate

▲ LOOKING WELL GROOMED

It is not always necessary to wear a suit, but it is always necessary to look well groomed. Make sure that your clothes are all clean and well pressed, your shoes are polished, and your hair is tidy.

▲ LOOKING UNKEMPT

If you do not take time to groom yourself, you will look unprepared, and the audience may assume that you are not an expert on your subject. An unkempt appearance may distract people from your message.

ENHANCING BODY IMAGE

As much as two thirds of communication between people is totally non-verbal, transmitted either through hand gestures, facial expressions, or other forms of body language. Good body image begins with posture – the way you hold your skeleton.

52 Make sure your body language reflects what you are saying.

ANALYZING YOUR STANCE

The best posture in which to begin your presentation is upright with the feet slightly apart, and the body weight divided equally between them. Your arms should be relaxed by your sides. This is the most non-committal posture and conveys neutral body language. You can build on this to create different impressions if you understand the ways in which various stances are interpreted. Leaning slightly forwards, for example, appears positive and friendly – as if you are involving and encouraging the audience. Leaning backwards, however, may appear negative and possibly aggressive.

53 Learn to relax your facial muscles – and smile!

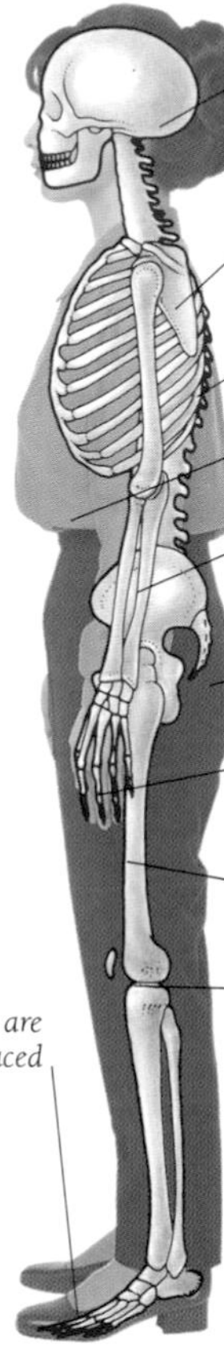

Head is held high and straight

Shoulders are pulled back and level

Back is straight

Stomach is held in

Arms are relaxed and hang by sides

Bottom is held in

Hands are relaxed; fingers are loose

Legs are straight

Knee joints are loose, not locked

Feet are evenly spaced

◀ **STANDING CORRECTLY**
Holding yourself upright and straight not only has physical benefits, such as improved vocal clarity, but can enhance your mental outlook as well. Standing properly increases your stature, which can give you greater self-confidence.

AVOIDING BAD HABITS

To improve your posture and avoid bad habits, practise in front of a mirror or video-tape your rehearsal, and watch for any unconscious mannerisms. Ask a colleague to watch you practising and comment on distracting gestures or stances.

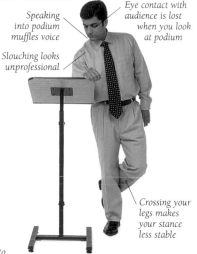

Eye contact with audience is lost when you look at podium

Speaking into podium muffles voice

Slouching looks unprofessional

Crossing your legs makes your stance less stable

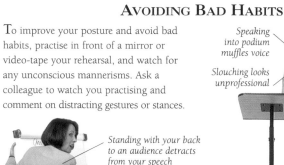

Standing with your back to an audience detracts from your speech

Visual aid blocked by body

◀ BLOCKING THE VIEW

Avoid the temptation to lean across visual aids as you use them. Prepare them in advance, and use a pointer so you do not block the audience's view.

▲ BEING UNBALANCED

Avoid standing on one leg or crossing your legs. These stances are unstable and also lack authority – an unbalanced body can be an indication of an unbalanced mind.

IMPROVING YOUR STANCE

The muscles in your body are there to hold the skeleton in an upright position. If you use them correctly, your body language will say "I am a well-balanced, confident person". If your muscles relax too much, your body will slouch. To improve your stance, practise standing in an upright position until you are confident that it looks and feels as natural as your usual relaxed standing position. Imagine that you are taller than you are, or that you are gently being pulled upwards by a thread leading from the top of your head, to help achieve and maintain this stance.

54 Always wear comfortable shoes when presenting.

55 Make sure your hair does not fall across your face.

IMPROVING YOUR VOICE

The tone and volume of your voice have a critical effect on a presentation. Understanding how the vocal system works, and how you can control it to manipulate the sound of your voice, is a key part of preparing yourself for a successful presentation.

56 Suck a mint or honey-flavoured sweet just before you begin to speak.

BREATHING CORRECTLY

Breathe slowly and deeply to improve the flow of oxygen into the body and thus the flow of blood to the brain. This will help you think more clearly, which, in turn, will help you order your thoughts when speaking in front of an audience. Taking in more oxygen also improves the flow of air to your vocal chords, allowing you to speak clearly, reducing nervousness, and helping you to remain calm.

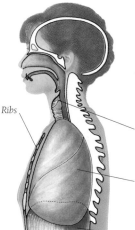

◀ **BREATHING FROM THE DIAPHRAGM**
Learning how to breathe from your diaphragm will give more support to your breathing and strengthen the pitch of your voice.

Ribs

Vocal chords produce sound when they vibrate as air passes over them

Lungs expand and contract with movement of ribs and diaphragm

Diaphragm separates chest from abdomen

57 Consider doing yoga exercises to improve the depth of your breathing.

CONTROLLING YOUR VOICE

Sound is produced when air passes over the vocal chords, making them vibrate. Thus the first requirement for speaking clearly is a good supply of air to the lungs. You can learn to improve your intake of air by practising a simple breathing exercise (see right). The second requirement is a properly functioning larynx, or voice box, which houses the vocal chords. Make an effort to rest your larynx the day before your presentation by limiting how much you speak.

USING THE RIGHT PITCH

In many languages, the only difference between asking a question and making a statement lies in the intonation. A statement such as "the managing director's office is over there" can be understood as a question if the pitch goes up at the end of the sentence. Your audience should understand the exact meaning of your words, so use intonation and pitch carefully to transmit the right message.

58 Practise changing the intonation of a few sentences.

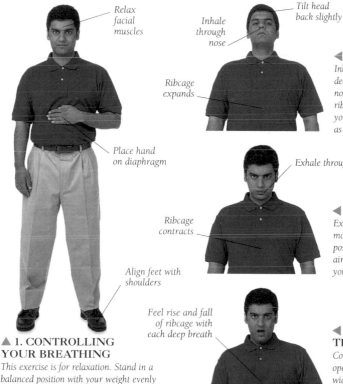

Relax facial muscles

Inhale through nose

Tilt head back slightly

◀ **2. INHALING**
Inhale slowly and deeply through the nose, feeling your ribcage expand. Hold your breath for as long as it is comfortable.

Ribcage expands

Place hand on diaphragm

Exhale through mouth

Ribcage contracts

◀ **3. EXHALING**
Exhale through the mouth as deeply as possible, pushing all the air out of your lungs as your ribcage contracts.

Align feet with shoulders

Feel rise and fall of ribcage with each deep breath

▲ **1. CONTROLLING YOUR BREATHING**
This exercise is for relaxation. Stand in a balanced position with your weight evenly distributed. Place your left hand on your diaphragm, listen to your breathing, and feel the rise and fall of your ribs as you breathe.

◀ **4. REPEATING THE EXERCISE**
Continue to exhale, opening your mouth widely as you do so. Repeat the exercise, pausing briefly between each breath taken.

ELIMINATING TENSION

When you are nervous your muscles become tense. This is because your body is preparing them in an instinctive way for "fight or flight", the basic choice people face when confronted with danger. Simple exercises can help to eliminate this tension.

> **59** Stretch yourself and imagine that you are taller than you really are.

REDUCING TENSION

Tension building up in your muscles can have some undesirable effects on your body during a presentation. Tension can spoil your posture, making you hunch your shoulders and look defensive. It can also prevent your larynx from functioning smoothly, giving your voice that familiar quiver identified with nervousness. Being tense for any length of time is tiring in itself and can detract from the impact of your presentation. By using a series of simple exercises to help reduce muscular tension, you can make sure that you have more control over your body.

Relieve tension in hand by gripping and relaxing

▲ HAND SQUEEZE
This simple exercise can be done anywhere at any time. Squeeze and release a small rubber ball in your hand. Repeat the exercise several times.

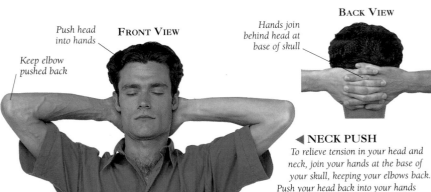

Push head into hands **FRONT VIEW**

Keep elbow pushed back

BACK VIEW

Hands join behind head at base of skull

◄ NECK PUSH
To relieve tension in your head and neck, join your hands at the base of your skull, keeping your elbows back. Push your head back into your hands as hard as you can. Hold this stretch for about 10 seconds, release, and repeat.

EXERCISING WHILE SEATED

It is possible to exercise even while you are sitting down – whether at your desk, stuck in a traffic jam, or at home. Follow the simple exercises below to keep your body supple and to help eliminate muscular tension. They do not require a high level of strength or fitness, and are most effective when practised on a daily basis. By taking the time to stretch your body for a couple of minutes each day, you can help prevent the onset of muscle tension and related conditions such as headaches, neckache, and backache.

60 Try to relax in an upright position for 10 minutes without moving.

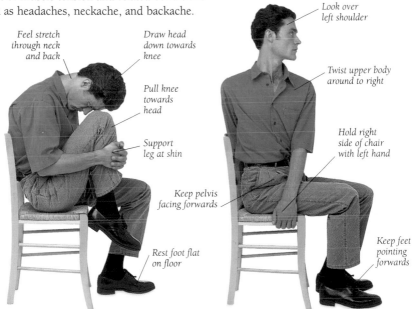

Feel stretch through neck and back

Draw head down towards knee

Pull knee towards head

Support leg at shin

Keep pelvis facing forwards

Rest foot flat on floor

Look over left shoulder

Twist upper body around to right

Hold right side of chair with left hand

Keep feet pointing forwards

▲ STRETCHING THE BODY

This stretch relieves tension in the neck, back, and hamstrings. Sit facing forwards in an upright chair, and pull your right knee towards your chest, supporting it with your hands joined across the shin. Lower your head, and hold the stretch for about 10 seconds. Repeat three times with each leg.

▲ STRETCHING THE SPINE

To relieve tension in your spine and shoulders while sitting down, hold the back of a chair seat with your right hand, turning to hold the right side of the chair with your left hand. Keeping your hips, legs, and feet facing forwards, look over your left shoulder. Hold for about 10 seconds, then repeat on the other side.

DELIVERING A PRESENTATION

The key to good delivery is to be yourself, to be natural. Anything else looks and sounds false – unless you have considerable acting talent.

CONTROLLING NERVES

All but the most experienced of speakers will feel nervous just before making a presentation. Nervousness prevents you from being natural, so you need to do everything you can to control your nerves in order to give the most effective presentation.

61 List the factors that make you nervous about presenting.

POINTS TO REMEMBER

- Checking that all your props and audio-visual aids have arrived at the venue enables you to concentrate on preparing yourself.
- Thorough preparation for your presentation should give you the confidence that everything is going to go right.
- Heavy eating or drinking before a presentation makes you feel and sound sleepy.
- Practice makes perfect.

IDENTIFYING NERVES

To deal with nerves effectively, you need to be able to anticipate and identify the signs of nerves that usually affect you. There are many symptoms; one of the most common is the feeling of having "butterflies in the stomach". Others signs include dryness of the mouth, the appearance of a twitch in the corner of an eye, trembling hands, sweaty palms, fidgeting with hair or clothing, and rocking from one side to the other, as well as general tension in various parts of the body. Everyone is affected differently, but it is quite common to experience more than one symptom at a time.

BEING PREPARED

One of the chief causes of nerves is the fear that something will go wrong during a presentation. By reducing the chances of this happening, you can minimize that fear, and your nerves will be calmer. The key is to prepare yourself thoroughly, and leave nothing to chance. Every time you think of something you wish to double-check, write it down. Accustom yourself to using a checklist each time you prepare to make a presentation. Some of the points you should remember to check are:

● That the pages of your script or notes are numbered, in case you drop them;
● That your AV aids will be understandable from the back of the venue;
● That all the electrical equipment you intend to use is functioning properly;
● That the venue and your appearance are confirmed, and that you have the right date.

> **62** Smile only when it feels natural to do so. A forced smile always looks false and unconvincing.

DEFUSING NERVES

To make a strong, effective presentation, you must be relaxed beforehand. Even if you do not feel tense, about 30 minutes before you are due to speak, try to find a quiet place to gather your thoughts and relax. If you know you do have a tendency to feel nervous, try to be positive about these feelings – in time they will become familiar, so welcome their arrival as if they were old friends, and try to use them. Rethink your attack of nerves – and rename it "anticipation".

PREPARATION
Remind yourself how thoroughly you did your preparation, and look through your notes for the presentation

REHEARSING
Remember the time you spent rehearsing the presentation, and reflect on what you learned during the rehearsals

RELAXATION
Work through your relaxation exercises five minutes before you begin – and meanwhile, relax

> **63** Get a good night's sleep the night before, so that you feel alert.

64 Follow the same last-minute routine before each speech.

65 Imagine yourself delivering a first-class speech.

ESTABLISHING A RITUAL

It can be helpful to follow a ritual in the last few minutes before you begin your presentation. This should come after the preparations described on the previous page, and should consist of taking a few moments to gather your thoughts, exercising the facial muscles as shown opposite, and doing a few breathing exercises. This should take your mind off the things that make you nervous. There is also something very comforting in following a sequence of undemanding actions before a stressful event. People who are afraid of flying find it helpful to follow a similar routine in the minutes before their plane takes off.

REASSURING YOURSELF

Before your presentation, reassure yourself by running through your last-minute calming ritual, and remind yourself of the following:

- Unless the waiting audience is hostile for some reason, remind yourself that people want to see a successful presentation. In other words, they are on your side;
- Despite the fact that most people are nervous before giving a speech, an audience will assume that you are not;
- You have a message to pass on to your audience – in the form of factual information, personal insights, or both. The audience wants to hear this message, otherwise they would not have given up the time to come and listen to your presentation. Take heart from this knowledge; use it to your advantage to boost your confidence and counteract your nerves;
- Be wary of being over-confident. This can make you sound like a know-all, and there are very few audiences, however interested in a topic, that will warm to such an individual.

POINTS TO REMEMBER

- Nerves can add extra, positive energy to your presentation.
- The audience is more interested in what you are saying than in how you are feeling.
- Your enthusiasm and sincerity will help win over the audience.
- A short exercise regime can help to reduce last-minute nerves.
- Time spent relaxing at the last minute helps you to concentrate during your presentation.
- The more presentations you make, the more opportunities you have to perfect your skills.

66 Use some of your nervous energy to enliven your speech.

ELIMINATING TENSION

Take time before you start your presentation to ease the tension that accumulates in the face and upper body. Rid your facial muscles of nervous tension by following the simple exercises shown below. This will help in the articulation of your presentation, as you will be less likely to trip over your tongue or stutter. Repeat all three exercises several times each, until your face feels relaxed.

67 Take a deep breath, relax, smile, and start your speech slowly.

Tense forehead muscles

Stretch jaw as wide as possible

Purse lips tightly together

Open eyes wide

▲ **FACIAL SQUEEZE**
Try to squeeze your face as though it is being compressed between your chin and forehead. Start with a frown. Relax and repeat.

▲ **FACIAL SCRUNCH**
Tightly close your eyes, purse your lips, and scrunch up your face as if there is sideways compression. Hold for 30 seconds, then relax.

▲ **MOUTH STRETCH**
Open both your eyes and mouth as wide as possible, stretching the muscles in your face. Repeat two or three times as required.

REDUCING LAST-MINUTE NERVES

Simple last-minute breathing exercises can help you reduce nerves by giving you better control over your body and voice. By concentrating on your breathing, you can also calm your thoughts and dispel feelings of tension and anxiety, enabling you to focus clearly. Follow the exercise on the right, shutting your eyes and taking a series of controlled, deep breaths.

Breathe in through nose

◀ **BREATHING EXERCISE**
Close your eyes. Place one hand on your upper chest, the other on your diaphragm. Breathe in, feeling your diaphragm rise, then breathe out slowly. Repeat several times.

Feel chest remain still as you inhale

Feel diaphragm rise with each inward breath

SPEAKING CONFIDENTLY

The delivery of a presentation has as much impact as the message itself. It is essential to start strongly. After that, use tone of voice, pace, and your body language to enhance your audience's understanding of what you have to say.

68 Scan your notes in small sections, then concentrate on fluent delivery.

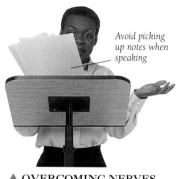

Avoid picking up notes when speaking

▲ OVERCOMING NERVES
Check the height of the lectern before you start a presentation to ensure it is at a comfortable level. If you feel nervous, it is tempting to hide behind your notes; train yourself to keep them on the lectern.

BEGINNING CONFIDENTLY

Make sure that you are introduced properly to the audience. A good introduction will establish your credibility and can provide the audience with a clear expectation of what you are about to tell them. Find out who will be introducing you, and brief them thoroughly. Make sure that your expertise in the subject of the presentation is mentioned if it would be helpful. Start speaking confidently and at a natural pace, and try to deliver your first few points without referring to your notes. This will reinforce an air of confidence, openness, and authority, and at the same time will enable you to establish eye contact with the audience. Try to glance at the whole audience at the start so that they feel involved.

PACING A PRESENTATION

Varying the pace of your delivery will keep the audience interested, but you should avoid speeding up and slowing down just for the sake of it. Remember to pause between your main points, and take the opportunity to make eye contact with the audience. This will also give you a chance to gauge their reactions to your speech. As you progress through the stages of your presentation, speak slowly and emphatically when you want to highlight important points.

69 Pause briefly each time you make an important point.

USING BODY LANGUAGE

At every moment of your waking life, you are sending out non-verbal signals about your feelings and intentions. It is possible to use this body language in a presentation to help to reinforce your message. Keep an open posture at all times, avoiding crossing your arms or creating a barrier between you and the audience. Use hand gestures selectively for emphasis – do not gesture so much that your hands become a distraction. If you are relaxed, your body language will reinforce your message naturally, but using the appropriate gestures can help you to disguise your nerves.

70 Tell a favourite, relevant anecdote; its familiarity will put you at ease.

Eye contact establishes positive rapport with audience

Relaxed body language conveys confidence

Open jacket presents an image of honesty

Gaze includes entire audience

Open hand gestures emphasize key points

▲ SPEAKING AUTHORITATIVELY
This confident stance suggests a thorough grasp of subject matter, and will establish authority and credibility with the audience.

▲ LOOKING AND FEELING RELAXED
Once audience rapport has been built, the speaker visibly relaxes and the audience focuses more readily on what is being said.

▲ USING THE RIGHT GESTURES
The speaker makes good use of open-handed gestures to emphasize his integrity and draw the entire audience into his presentation.

USING EYE CONTACT

Eye contact is a very powerful tool that establishes a degree of intimacy between people. It is important to establish this intimacy with an audience during a presentation. Sweep your gaze right across the audience, remembering to engage with the people at the very back and far sides, as well as those at the front. Although it is tempting to increase the frequency of eye contact with audience members who appear enthusiastic and interested, do not neglect those who appear neutral or negative. Audience members who feel excluded by the speaker are more likely to respond negatively to the speech than those who feel involved.

LOOKING AT THE AUDIENCE ▶

Sweep your gaze across the entire audience, remembering to include the back row. Establish initial eye contact with a friendly face, rather than looking over the heads of your audience when speaking.

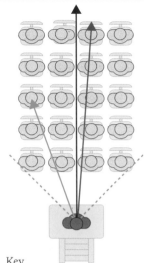

Key

---- *Limit of speaker's sightlines*

→ *Sightline fixed on friendly face in audience*

→ *Sightline fixed on back row of audience*

➤ *Sightline fixed on middle distance*

> **71** Make your initial eye contact with someone whom you consider to look approachable.

USING GESTURES

Perspective changes in relation to the size of the audience, and you have to adapt your gestures accordingly. Large audiences require greatly exaggerated movements to achieve the same visual effect that a "normal" gesture would for a small audience. For example, a gesture emphasizing two points "on the one hand...and on the other hand..." needs to start from the shoulder, rather than from the elbow or wrist, to have the right visual impact on a large audience. Although gesturing in this exaggerated style may at first feel awkward, it will look natural to the audience.

72 Make eye contact with somebody in the audience at every available opportunity.

DEVELOPING STYLE

As you become more experienced you will be able to use the various tools you have at your disposal – your voice, your demeanour, and the words you use – to create different impressions. Usually you will want to use all the tools at the same time to work towards the single goal of keeping the attention of the audience. For example, if you want to emphasize a point, use concise sentences, stand upright, and raise your voice. To give the audience the impression that you are going to share an exciting revelation with them, lean forwards and lower your voice. They will make sure that they hear you because you have made it seem so interesting. These tools are an essential element of any presenter's success, and with practice their use will become second nature. Always use a style that is appropriate to each particular audience – what works well for one group of people may not work at all with another.

73 Repeat key numbers: "15 – one-five – weeks."

74 Do not be afraid to use big gestures and long pauses.

LIMITING YOUR SPEECH TIME

Tell your audience how long you will be speaking for so they know how long they need to concentrate: "We've only got 20 minutes, so let me go straight in…". Later you can remind them again that your eye is still on the clock: "We've only got five minutes left, so I'll sum up by saying…". Do not be diverted from your prepared presentation by a member of the audience who wishes to ask a question or appears to disagree with a point you are making. Tell them when you will be answering questions from the floor, and continue your speech.

DO'S AND DON'TS

☑ Do use simple, concise language wherever possible, for clarity.

☑ Do use eye contact to obtain feedback from the audience. Their body language will reveal their reactions to your presentation.

☑ Do keep pauses specific and emphatic. Use them to allow your audience to absorb what you say.

☑ Do glance at a wall clock to check on the time rather than looking at your watch.

☒ Don't apologize to the audience for your lack of speaking experience.

☒ Don't mumble or hesitate. If you have lost your place, stay calm until you find it.

☒ Don't drop your voice at the end of a each sentence. It will sound as if you are not sure of what you are saying.

☒ Don't lose sight of the message that you are giving, or you will find that you lose your concentration as well as your audience.

CLOSING EFFECTIVELY

It is vital to have a strong conclusion to your presentation, since this helps form the impression that audience members take away with them. Always reiterate the major points made in your speech to bring them to the attention of the audience again.

75 Do not leave visual aids on display too long – they distract the audience.

SIGNPOSTING THE END

During the course of your presentation, give the audience verbal signposts to indicate how many more points you have to make, and when the end of your speech is approaching. Use phrases such as: "now the third of my four points…" or "and now, to sum up briefly before I answer your questions…". By informing the audience that the end is near, you will be sure of having their full attention before you summarize your main points. It is important that your summary covers all the major points and ideas from your presentation, so that the audience has a final chance to recap on your subject matter. This gives them a chance to consider any questions that they want to ask you.

THINGS TO DO

1. Tell the audience how many points you want them to take away with them.
2. Make sure you stick to your allocated time.
3. Work out which points can be cut if you run over your allotted time.
4. If you forget anything, leave it out rather than adding it to the end of your speech.

76 Do not rush off as if you are in a hurry to leave.

77 Always close with a good, strong summary.

LEAVING AN IMPRESSION

It is the final impression that you leave in the minds of your audience that lingers the longest, so make sure that it is a good one. Before delivering the presentation, spend time working on the final sentences of it so that you can deliver them perfectly. Combine pauses, intonation, and verbal devices such as alliteration in your summary to create a memorable "package" for the audience to take away with them. In this way, your message will get across – and your reputation as a speaker will be enhanced.

Drawing to a Close

Use open hand gestures to show enthusiasm

Avoid adopting a dogmatic tone when delivering the conclusion to your presentation. Concentrate on presenting accurate, well-researched facts, and do not be tempted into giving personal opinions on your subject matter. Base your conclusion firmly on the facts you have presented throughout your speech. If your presentation is to be followed by a question-and-answer session, remember that the impact of your own carefully prepared final sentences may be diluted. In such a case, you may choose to accept a series of questions from the audience and then make a short, concise summing up speech reiterating your major points.

DELIVERING YOUR SUMMARY ▶
As you are about to begin summing up your presentation, move to the front of any visual aids you are using so that the audience can see you clearly. Stand confidently, and deliver your closing sentences authoritatively.

78 Use alliteration to make an impact when summing up.

79 Pause between your summary and the question-and-answer session.

Finishing Strongly

It is important to create a strong and memorable finish. To help you to do this, there are several tips that you should bear in mind:

- Encapsulate your presentation in one or two sentences. It is important to be brief when summing up; short, powerful sentences hold the attention of the audience far more effectively than a 10-minute monologue;
- Emphasize key words. Pausing after key words and phrases adds emphasis to them. It is also a good idea to emphasize the word "and" as you approach your final main point;
- Use alliteration. The use of several words beginning with the same letter helps make a summary memorable. Restrict the alliteration to a maximum of three words.

HANDLING AN AUDIENCE

A presentation is made for the benefit of an audience, not for that of the presenter. Be sure that you know how to read an audience's response and how to handle its reactions.

JUDGING THE MOOD

Try to arrive at the venue early enough to assess the mood of the audience. Has the audience just come in from the pouring rain? Are they likely to be hostile to what you want to tell them? Has a previous speaker made them laugh?

80 Listen to as many of the previous speakers as you possibly can.

INVOLVING AN AUDIENCE

Judge the mood of your audience – by assessing their reactions to previous speakers, for example. You can then decide on a strategy to deliver your message effectively. If any members of the audience appear bored or drowsy, stimulate them by asking questions that can be answered by a show of hands. "How many of you phoned your office before coming here? Only three? Well then, how many of you *thought* of phoning your office?" If the audience is hostile, you could start the presentation with a joke, but make sure that your body language is giving out positive signals.

81 Let audience members know that you are aware of their feelings.

LOOKING FOR SIGNALS

You will have rehearsed your own body language as part of your preparations for a presentation. Now you have to learn to read the body language of the members of the audience. Watch for signs, and do not expect everyone to be expressing the same thing. Some may be straining forwards eagerly to ask a question, while others may be sinking into their seats, wishing they were somewhere else.

82 Involve members of the audience by asking questions at regular intervals.

Impassive expression

Folded arms form a barrier across body

Crossed legs can suggest negativity

NEGATIVE ▶ POSTURE
This posture – leaning back with arms folded and legs crossed – suggests resistance towards the presenter.

SPOTTING NEGATIVITY

There is a wide range of ways in which members of an audience can indicate disapproval or hostility. Watch out for people leaning over and criticizing your speech to a neighbour. Alternatively, look for people frowning directly at you with their arms folded, or looking in the air as if the ceiling is more interesting than anything you have to say. Remember that looking at one piece of body language in isolation – such as crossed legs – may give a false impression, so look at the whole picture before coming to a conclusion.

SEEING SIGNS OF INTEREST

Stances indicating interest are easy to spot – look for people smiling or nodding, or leaning forwards in their seats and watching you intently. The expressions on their faces may reveal faint frowns of concentration. People manifesting any of these signs can probably be won over to your point of view, so make sure that you involve or engage them in your presentation.

Frown of concentration

Torso leans forwards

Clasped fingers indicate thoughtfulness

◀ QUIZZICAL POSTURE
Leaning forwards, with elbows on knees, and chin resting on clasped hands, suggests that this person is considering a point that the speaker is making.

READING FACIAL SIGNS

In terms of body language, the face is most expressive. If you are close enough to the members of your audience, you will be able to pick up a multitude of small signals – from the movements of eyebrows and the look in the eyes to the sloping of lips. As with general body language, always remember to read the face as a whole. One sign taken in isolation may not be a true indication of what the person is feeling.

83 Watch for a hand stealthily moving up to stifle a yawn.

Neutral facial expression indicates unformed opinions

Chin resting on hand shows concentration

Crossed legs suggest contemplation

NEUTRAL ▶ POSTURE

This familiar relaxed posture suggests an open mind. This person has yet to be swayed either way by the argument and is willing to hear more.

READING HAND AND ARM GESTURES

Hand and arm movements are helpful in adding to the impact of speech and can tell you a lot about the person using them. During question-and-answer sessions, note the hand and arm gestures of the people asking questions. If you cannot see them clearly, ask individuals to stand up when speaking. The gestures people use have a strong cultural content, so bear this in mind when interpreting body language. For example, if northern Europeans gesticulate emphatically, they are probably agitated, but such gesturing accompanies most conversations among southern Europeans.

DEALING WITH UNFORESEEN CIRCUMSTANCES

Would you know what to do if there was a loud explosion in the middle of your presentation? Or if a member of the audience suddenly had a seizure? Although the chances of such an event are remote, it is as well to go over in your mind the steps you might follow if you were faced with an unexpected incident such as this. Ask yourself if you know where to turn on the lights, where to find a first-aid kit, how to summon medical help, and where the fire exits are. If you do not know where you might find these things, make sure you get this information before your presentation.

USING YOUR EARS

You do not need to have all the lights on to pick up your audience's body language; much of it can be picked up aurally. You can hear the rustle of people fidgeting or the sound of whispering, both of which may indicate that your audience is bored or confused. It is easy to block yourself off when you are concentrating on presenting, but it pays to be alert to noise at all times – it is a valuable clue for judging the mood of your audience.

84 Be aware of tapping feet – a strong indication of impatience.

WATCHING LEGS

The position into which someone puts their legs says a lot about their attitude. For example, if an audience member has crossed legs, it may indicate that they are still contemplating your speech. Legs placed together, however, can indicate total agreement. If your audience is seated, movement will be limited and you may be able to see only those in the front row, but their leg movements should give you an indication of how the rest of the audience are reacting to your presentation.

Position of chin on knuckles indicates eagerness to learn

Arrangement of legs indicates alertness

◀ **INTERESTED POSTURE**
This posture expresses interest. The body leans forwards, and the chin rests on the hand. The leg positions also reinforce the positive stance of the upper body.

Leaning forwards demonstrates agreement

AGREEMENT ▶ POSTURE
The relaxed position of the hands, the parallel legs, and the frank, open expression of the face indicate that the listener agrees entirely with your presentation.

NOTICING HABITS

Most people unintentionally reinforce their body language with habitual fidgeting with their personal props, such as glasses, watches, earrings, or cufflinks. Looking at a watch can betray boredom or even impatience, while chewing on a pen or glasses suggests contemplation. On the positive side, sitting still and an absence of any of these habits can often indicate total involvement and agreement with the content of your presentation.

DEALING WITH QUESTIONS

Many a fine presentation has been ruined by poor handling of questions raised by the audience afterwards. Learn to deal with difficult and awkward questions during your preparation, and you will handle anything you are asked with confidence.

85 Practise answering some impromptu questions put to you by a friend.

86 Remain calm, whatever the tone or intention of the questioner.

POINTS TO REMEMBER

- Question-and-answer sessions can be as important as the main body of the presentation itself.
- It is possible to anticipate most questions when researching presentation material thoroughly.
- Most questions taken from the audience will be intended generally, and should not be taken personally.
- Nerves may tempt you to a hasty response. Always think about your answer before you begin to speak.
- Some questions may need clarification from the questioner.
- Questions should always be answered one at a time.

PREPARING WELL

It is important that you go into your presentation fully prepared to answer any questions thrown at you by the audience. The key to this is in careful research and rewriting. Once you have finished drafting your speech, read it through thoroughly several times, note any unanswered questions that it raises, and try to fill in any gaps. Having done this, read your presentation to friends or colleagues, and ask them to raise any queries. Deal with their points, adding extra information as necessary. Be aware that, despite this preparation, there may be somebody who asks an awkward question you have not thought of.

APPEARING CONFIDENT

Just as a good presentation can be ruined by a poor question-and-answer session, a mediocre one can be saved by a confident performance at the end. Answer questions as loudly, clearly, and succinctly as you delivered the presentation. This is especially important if you have had to sit down or move to another location for questioning. If appropriate, stand up when answering questions, and keep your voice level. Do not fidget with your hands or use negative body language, such as crossing your arms in front of your chest, which will make you appear defensive.

STAYING IN CONTROL

Never allow more than one person to talk at once, otherwise the occasion may rapidly head out of control. Establish that you can only handle one question at a time: "If we could hear your question first, John, then I'll come back to you, Laura, immediately afterwards". Never be drawn into a protracted discussion of minor aspects of your presentation; if matters become too involved, arrange to continue the discussion afterwards.

 87 Say "Good point!" to encourage a questioner who is shy or nervous.

 88 Divert hostile questions back to the questioner or the audience.

HANDLING QUESTIONERS

Questioners come in a variety of guises, so it is important to be able to recognize and deal with them accordingly. Exhibitionists like to try and demonstrate that they know more than you do, while drifters wander around the subject and never seem to ask a direct question. Each requires careful handling. Bring the drifter back to the issue by saying, "That's a good point, and it raises a question about...". Exhibitionists may cause trouble if antagonized, so treat them politely at all times.

TYPES OF QUESTION TO EXPECT FROM AN AUDIENCE

There are certain typical queries that come up over and over in question-and-answer sessions. Learn to recognize these so that you can deal with them successfully:

- The Summary Question: "What you seem to be saying is... Am I right?" This is an effort to recap on proceedings.
- The Straight Question: "Can you tell me about the services you offer in Brazil?" This is a direct appeal for information.
- The Me and Mine Question: "When my mother tried, she found the opposite.

How do you explain that?" Personal experience is used to make a point.

- The Cartesian Question: "How can you say X, yet insist on Y?" Here logic is being used to defeat the speaker.
- The Raw Nerve Question: "When are you going to get back to 1995 levels?" This is an ill-natured dig.
- The Well-Connected Question: "Have you talked to my good friend Bill Clinton about this problem?" Name dropping is used to emphasize power.

ANALYZING QUESTIONS

You only have a brief moment to analyze the nature of each question you are asked. Are you being asked to recap on your presentation? Is it a simple request for further information on your subject matter? Are you being led into a trap? Some people want to make a point rather than ask a question – if their input is positive and reinforces your argument, it is courteous to acknowledge them. However, if the point is irrelevant, thank the speaker and move on to the next question.

GAINING TIME

If you find yourself faced with a particularly difficult question, remain calm and give yourself a little time to think carefully before you reply. When tackling a question that requires careful thought, do not be afraid to refer back to your notes – you will still appear to be in control if you tell the audience what you are doing and why. If absolutely necessary, use a stalling tactic, such as taking a sip of water, coughing, or blowing your nose. This will help you to avoid looking as though you are lost for words.

89 Address answers to the whole audience, not just the questioner.

POINTS TO REMEMBER

- Answering questions from the audience can increase your credibility by demonstrating a wider knowledge of your subject.
- The audience needs to know whether you are voicing personal opinions or facts.
- It is crucial not to be drawn into argument with a questioner, regardless of how unacceptable his or her assumptions are.
- All questions should be handled with respect and courtesy.
- Some really difficult questions may have to be researched and answered at a later date.

RESPONDING TO UNANSWERABLE QUESTIONS

There are a number of standard replies you can use in response to difficult questions. If you do not know an answer, try to offer a satisfactory reply to show you have not ignored the question. If a questioner persists, throw the question open to the audience.

❝ *I don't know the answer, but I can find out for you. If you leave me your address, I will get back to you.* ❞

❝ *I need to think about that one. Could we come back to it later? Next question, please.* ❞

❝ *I'm not sure I know the answer to that one. Perhaps we could discuss it after the session.* ❞

❝ *There really is no right or wrong answer to that. However, my personal belief is...* ❞

DEALING WITH HIDDEN AGENDAS

Beware of loaded questions designed to show up serious weaknesses in an argument, embarrass the speaker, and undermine your case. Questions that have little to do with your presentation may be an attempt by a member of the audience to show off. Alternatively, they may stem from a desire to destroy your credibility by making you appear ill-informed. Try to have a few stock answers at your disposal, such as: "I was not intending to cover that aspect of the subject today", or "That is a separate issue that I do not have time to discuss now", which, though evasive, will ease the pressure on you.

90 Win over your audience with your knowledge.

91 Take care not to patronize your audience.

SPEAKING OFF THE CUFF

On occasions, you may find that somebody in the audience asks a probing question that needs a great deal of discussion about one aspect of your presentation. If this is not of general interest, ask the questioner to contact you after your presentation has finished. However, if you feel that the entire audience would benefit from hearing more detail – and you are sure of your facts – you may chose to launch into an unrehearsed mini-presentation. Keeping it brief, structure your impromptu speech clearly, and present it as fluently as the main body of the presentation.

BEING HONEST WITH THE AUDIENCE

There are going to be times when, for various reasons, you simply do not know the answer to a question. If this happens, be honest with the audience. If you do not know the facts, it is best to admit this straight away rather than hedging around the issue. Do not respond with phrases like "I will be covering that point later", because the audience will resent any attempt to fool them, and you may lose credibility.

Assess whether the required reply is purely factual or also a matter of personal opinion. If it is the latter, you are on firmer ground, since you can admit to not knowing the facts but still give a reasonable and considered answer based on past experience or personal opinion.

92 Prepare one or two lengthy answers in advance for questions you are sure will be raised.

COPING WITH HOSTILITY

A presentation may occasionally give rise to strong feelings or violently opposed viewpoints among members of the audience. When faced with such a situation, you must be able to cope with both overt outbursts of hostility and a silent reception.

93 Remember that hostility is aimed at your opinions, not at you.

94 Avoid prolonged eye contact; it may cause aggravation.

RECOGNIZING DISRUPTERS

Learn to recognize the types of disruptive audience members you may face, and you will be able to deal with them more effectively. Attention-seekers may respond to a speech with sarcasm just to make themselves look clever, while others may respond unwittingly to a rhetorical question, for example, without intending you any malice. The most disruption is likely to be caused by hecklers in the audience – people who disagree with what you are saying, and who actively want to cause trouble.

Illuminate points with interesting example

Sum up main points so far

Pause to take a drink of water, and renew eye contact since this can change the course of events

Start off strongly

Drop notes on floor

Tell a joke at your own expense

Heckler shouts "Rubbish!"

Presentation degenerates into chaos

DEALING WITH HECKLERS

Hecklers appear in all sorts of situations, harassing speakers with awkward comments and interruptions. To deal with hecklers you must be polite but firm. Your goal should be to get the rest of the audience on your side. This is not always easy, and underestimating hecklers can be costly if you allow them to undermine your presentation. Hecklers often have a genuine concern, which, if not addressed properly and quickly, may be taken up by other members of the audience.

If someone denounces something that you have said, do not enter an argument with them. If you are stating fact rather than opinion, make this clear and present the evidence. If you are stating personal opinion, be frank about it; this is your presentation. Give hecklers an opportunity to speak afterwards.

POINTS TO REMEMBER

- Losing your temper will gain you nothing.
- Everyone deserves a fair hearing even if you cannot agree with their point of view.
- Any points of agreement with hecklers should be emphasized.
- It is important to repeat your case at the end of the presentation.

 95 If you are stating facts, back them up with evidence.

Respond well to questions from audience

Conclude with clear summary

▲ KEEPING ON TRACK

This illustration shows two possible courses of a presentation – a negative outcome and positive outcome. Despite a strong start, there may be hecklers and mishaps. This could cause a presentation to end in chaos. To stay on course, stay calm, deal with mishaps as they occur, and move on with composure and aplomb. Hold the audience's interest and you can make a success of any situation.

DEALING WITH CONFLICT WITHIN AN AUDIENCE

If a serious disagreement between members of an audience disrupts your presentation, remember that you will be assumed by the audience to be the mediator. Defuse the tension by reassuring everyone that they will get a chance to speak, and restore equilibrium as soon as possible. Get everyone back on to the right path by reminding the audience of the presentation's purpose. In all cases, aim to convey to your audience that you are in control. If the situation deteriorates any further, enlist some help from the organizers, or bring the presentation to an end.

 96 If you are giving your presentation sitting down, stand up in order to assert your authority.

97 Try to find some common ground with the audience.

98 Guide questioners to other sources of information.

FACING AN UNRESPONSIVE GROUP

Although an unresponsive audience is not necessarily a hostile audience, many people would prefer to deal with outright hostility than silence. In such a situation, it is easy to imagine that the audience has no questions because there is no interest in your talk. This is unlikely to be the case – they are probably just unresponsive people. If a chairperson is present, you should have no worries. He or she will invite questions from the audience and, if there are none, start with questions of their own. If there is no chairperson, try asking the audience a few general, direct questions to encourage them to respond to you.

DEALING WITH HOSTILITY

An audience might be hostile for a number of reasons, including fundamental disagreement with the point of your presentation, anger at a previous speaker, or resentment at having to sit through your speech when they really came to hear someone else. One technique you can use to deal with hostility is to acknowledge it. Try to disarm a hostile audience by being open, then ask them to be fair and non-judgmental while you give your presentation. Another possibility is to plant a friend or colleague in the audience with a question with which to open the discussion. Your "plant" can ask an apparently awkward question, to which you can respond with a strong, preplanned answer – winning over some audience members.

99 Wait for questions, even if there are none forthcoming.

CULTURAL DIFFERENCES

Sometimes a speaker can unwittingly generate hostility in an audience by making a cultural *faux pas*. When making a presentation, pointing with the index finger to emphasize a remark is considered acceptable by most Westerners. However, many Asians cultures consider this rude, and prefer gestures of indication to be made with the whole hand.

100 Tell the truth, because an audience will quickly recognize insincerity and your authority will be undermined.

DEALING WITH THE MEDIA

If you have to speak at a public meeting or represent your organization at a press conference, it is important to handle the media confidently. Always answer queries calmly, politely, and intelligently, and be careful not to let journalists put words into your mouth.

❝ *I have already stated my point of view during my presentation. I don't think I have anything more to add at this juncture…* ❞

❝ *No, that is not what I am saying at all. I would like to reiterate that what I am actually saying is…* ❞

❝ *You have certainly made a valid point, but I prefer to think that…* ❞

❝ *Whereas I appreciate what you are saying, I feel that I must emphasize that…* ❞

LEARNING FROM YOUR EXPERIENCE

Dealing with awkward questions and general hostility during a presentation requires skills that can take a long time to develop. Learn from your mistakes, and draw on other situations in life when you have been faced with such difficulties. How did you cope? Did you think the situation through before responding? Did you defuse the situation tactfully? What if an audience resorts to derisive laughter in an attempt to undermine your credibility? The best response in this situation is to employ humour – never use sarcasm, which may only serve to exacerbate the situation.

If you know that your presentation is likely to provoke antagonism – for example, when making an unwelcome speech to shareholders or at a public meeting – try to anticipate the hostility. Practise fielding aggressive comments successfully by asking colleagues to fire difficult questions at you. The more experience you have, the better you will become at responding confidently.

POINTS TO REMEMBER

● Remaining calm when faced with hostility from the audience can help defuse a negative situation.

● Only the question that has been asked should be answered, not one that you would have preferred.

● Answers should be kept relatively short, especially if you know that there are other questioners waiting to be heard.

● There may be a hidden agenda behind aggression or hostility.

● Silence can be used to provoke an audience to ask questions.

 101 Stay relaxed but alert, and enjoy your presentation.

ASSESSING YOUR ABILITY

Remember that practice makes perfect when preparing for a presentation: regard each presentation as a chance to practise for the next. Evaluate your performance by responding to the following statements, and mark the options closest to your experience. Be as honest as you can: if your answer is "never", mark Option 1; if it is "always", mark Option 4; and so on. Add your scores together, and refer to the Analysis to see how you scored. Use your answers to identify the areas that need improving.

OPTIONS
1 Never
2 Occasionally
3 Frequently
4 Always

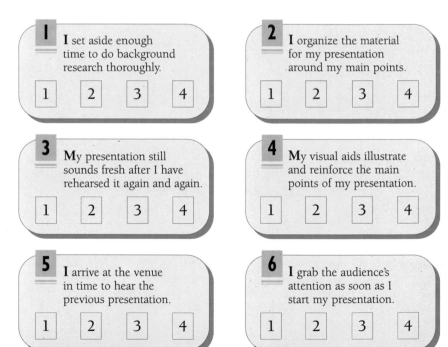

1 I set aside enough time to do background research thoroughly.

1   2   3   4

2 I organize the material for my presentation around my main points.

1   2   3   4

3 My presentation still sounds fresh after I have rehearsed it again and again.

1   2   3   4

4 My visual aids illustrate and reinforce the main points of my presentation.

1   2   3   4

5 I arrive at the venue in time to hear the previous presentation.

1   2   3   4

6 I grab the audience's attention as soon as I start my presentation.

1   2   3   4

7 I speak at a volume and pace that appears to suit the audience.

| 1 | 2 | 3 | 4 |

8 I speak fluently and confidently throughout the presentation.

| 1 | 2 | 3 | 4 |

9 I make eye contact with all sections of my audience throughout the presentation.

| 1 | 2 | 3 | 4 |

10 My presentation interests the audience and provokes questions from them.

| 1 | 2 | 3 | 4 |

11 I remain calm when responding to awkward or hostile questioners.

| 1 | 2 | 3 | 4 |

12 My replies are to the point and hold the interest of the audience.

| 1 | 2 | 3 | 4 |

ANALYSIS

Now you have completed the self-assessment, add up your total score and check your performance by reading the corresponding evaluation. Whatever level of success you have achieved during your presentation, it is important to remember that there is always room for improvement. Identify your weakest areas, and refer to the sections in this book where you will find practical advice and tips to help you establish and hone those skills.

12–24: Use every opportunity to learn from your mistakes, and take more time to prepare and rehearse for each presentation that you give from now on.

25–36: Your presentation skills are generally sound, but certain areas need improvement.

37–48: You have good presentation skills, but do not become complacent. Continue to prepare well.

INDEX

A

abilities, assessing your, 7
acoustics, of venues, 13, 15
advertising presentations, 13
agendas, 13
aims, considering your, 6
alliteration, using, 55
anecdotes, 18, 24, 51
appearance:
  avoiding bad habits, 41
  hair, 39, 41
  making an impression, 38
  posture, 40, 41
  unkempt, 39
  well-groomed, 39
arms, see gestures
attention span, of audience, 19, 24
audience:
  attention span of, 19, 24
  body language of, 53, 57–59
  boredom of, 7, 56, 59
  communicating with, 26
  creative visualization of, 37
  encouraging responses from, 18
  evaluating, 8–9
  eye contact with, 50, 52
  feedback from, 35, 53
  handling of, 56–65
  hostility from, 7, 57, 64–67
  how you appear to, 38
  interaction with, 9
  introduction to, 50
  inviting, 13
  question-and-answer sessions, 13, 55, 60–63
  reassuring yourself about, 48
  seating, 16
  size of, 9, 32
audio systems, 31
audio-visual (AV) aids, 30–33
  breakdown of, 7
autocues, 29

B

back, reducing tension in, 45
bad habits, avoiding, 41
body image, 40–41

body language:
  audience's, 53, 57–59
  faces, 58
  hands and arms, 58
  legs, 59
  habits, 41, 59
  in question-and-answer sessions, 60
  using, 40, 41, 51

C

cards, notes on, 28, 29
CD-ROMs, 31
chairperson, 12
  of group presentations, 13
  question-and-answer sessions, 13
  handling unresponsive audiences, 66
chairs, seating plans, 16
charts, 31
checklists, 12
clarifying objectives, 18–19
closing a presentation, 25, 54–55
clothes, 38–39
computers:
  graphics, 31, 32
  Internet, the, 21
  teleprompts, 29
  writing scripts on, 29
confidence:
  speaking confidently, 50–53
  believing in yourself, 36–37
  creative visualization, 37
  question-and-answer sessions, 60
  rehearsals, 34, 35
conflict, within audience, 65
creative visualization, 37
cultural differences, 66

D

design elements, in audio-visual aids, 33

E

emergencies, 58
ending a presentation, 25, 54–55
energy, harnessing, 49
enthusiasm, 19

equipment:
  audio-visual aids, 30–33
  breakdown of, 7
  microphones, 17
evaluating an audience, 8–9
exercises:
  breathing, 42, 43, 49
  facial, 49
  reducing tension, 44–45, 49
  stretching, 44–45
  while seated, 45
eye contact, 52
  in creative visualization, 37
  with audience, 9, 50
  with hecklers, 64

F

faces:
  reading audience's, 58
  reducing tension in, 49
fears, reducing, 7, 47
feedback, from audience, 35
flip-charts, 30, 31

G

gestures, 40, 51
  audience's hand and arm, 58
  exaggerating, 52
  rehearsing, 35
grammar, 26
group presentations, 13

H

hair, 39, 41
handouts, 30, 32
hands:
  reducing tension in, 44
  see also gestures
headphones, 31
heating, in venue, 15
hecklers, 7, 64–65
hidden agendas, 63
hostile audiences, 7
  body language of, 57
  coping with, 64–67

I

impressions:
  final, 54
  first, 38

information:
    prioritizing levels of, 27
    researching, 20–21
    selecting key points, 19
    summing up, 25
interaction with audience, 9
interest, seeing signs of, 57
Internet, the, 21
intonation, using, 43
introductions, importance of, 50
inviting an audience, 13

J
jet-lag, 11
jokes, 18, 56

K
key points, 19
    background research, 20
    emphasizing, 25, 50
    structuring, 22–23
key words, in summing up, 55

L
laser pointers, 33
lecterns, 50
lights, dimming, 14
linking ideas, 25
logistics, 10–13

M
media, dealing with, 67
metaphors, using, 23
microphones, 17, 31
mood, of audience, 56
multimedia, 31, 32
muscles:
    posture, 41
    reducing tension in, 44–45

N
narrative techniques, 23
neck, reducing tension in,
    44, 45
negative reactions, of
    audience, 57
nerves:
    controlling, 7, 46–49
    eliminating nervous tension,
        44–45
non-verbal communication,
    40, 51
notes:
    cards, 29
    hiding behind, 50
    preparing, 28, 29

O
objectives, clarifying, 18–19
opening remarks, 24, 50
outlines, structuring material, 24
overhead projectors, 31, 33

P
pacing presentations, 28, 50
pauses, 28, 50
pitch, of voice, 34, 43
positive thinking, 36
posture:
    analyzing, 40
    of audience, 57
    improving, 41
    reducing tension, 44
    using body language, 51
preparing:
    presentation, 6–35
    yourself, 36–45
press conferences, 67
press-cuttings agencies, 20
projectors:
    overhead, 31, 33
    slide, 30
prompt cards, 29
publicity, 13

Q
question-and-answer sessions,
    55, 60–63
    group presentations, 13
    hostile audiences, 67
    silent audiences, 66

R
rating your performance, 68–69
reassuring yourself, 48
recapping, 25
reference material, 20
rehearsing, 34–35
reinforcing key points, 25
relaxation:
    exercises, 44–45, 49
    reassuring yourself, 48
repetition, 25
research, 20–21
    sources, 20
    using new technology, 21
rituals, last-minute, 48
rough drafts, 28

S
seating:
    audience, 16
    adapting to venue, 17

self-image, 36
sentences:
    structure, 26, 27
    summing up, 55
shoes, 39, 41
shoulders, reducing tension in, 45
signposts, verbal, 54
silence, question-and-answer
    sessions, 66
slide projectors, 30
smiling, 47, 67
spine, reducing tension in, 45
spontaneity, 34
stalling tactics, using in
    question-and-answer
    sessions, 62
stance, see posture
streamlining material, 27
structuring material, 18, 22–25
style, developing, 53
summing up, 25, 54, 55
syntax, 26

T
tension, eliminating, 44–45
thinking positively, 36
timing:
    length of speech, 53
    pacing a speech, 28
tone of presentation, 18
tone of voice, 25
travel, planning, 11

U
unforeseen circumstances, 58
unresponsive audiences, 66

V
venues:
    acoustics of, 13, 15
    adapting to your needs, 17
    assessing, 14–17
video, 30, 33
visual aids, see audio-visual aids
visualization, creative, 37
vocal chords, 42
voice, 42–43
    controlling, 35, 42
    pitch of, 34, 43
    reducing tension in, 44
    tone of, 25

W
World Wide Web, 21
writing a presentation, 26–29
writing boards, 30, 31, 32

ACKNOWLEDGMENTS

AUTHOR'S ACKNOWLEDGMENTS

The production of this book has called on the skills of many people. I would like particularly to mention my editors at Dorling Kindersley, and my assistant Jane Williams.

PUBLISHER'S ACKNOWLEDGMENTS

Dorling Kindersley would like to thank Emma Lawson for her valuable part in the planning and development of this series, everyone who generously lent props for the photoshoots, and the following for their help and participation:

Editorial Tracey Beresford, Marian Broderick, Anna Cheifetz, Michael Downey, Jane Garton, Adèle Hayward, Catherine Rubinstein; **Design** Helen Benfield, Darren Hill, Ian Midson, Kate Poole, Simon J. M. Oon, Nicola Webb, Ellen Woodward; **DTP assistance** Rachel Symons; **Consultants** Josephine Bryan, Jane Lyle; **Indexer** Hilary Bird; **Proofreader** David Perry; **Photography** Steve Gorton; **Additional photography** Andy Crawford, Tim Ridley; **Photographers' assistants** Sarah Ashun, Nick Goodall, Lee Walsh; **Illustrators** Joanna Cameron, Yahya El-Droubie, Richard Tibbetts.

Models Carole Evans, Vosjava Fahkro, John Gillard, Ben Glickman, Zahid Malik, Sotiris Melioumis, Mutsumi Niwa, Ted Nixon, Mary-Jane Robinson, Lois Sharland, Gilbert Wu; **Make-up** Elizabeth Burrage.

Special thanks to the following for their help throughout the series:
Ron and Chris at Clark Davis & Co. Ltd for stationery and furniture supplies; Pam Bennett and the staff at Jones Bootmakers, Covent Garden, for the loan of footwear; Alan Pfaff and the staff at Moss Bros, Covent Garden, for the loan of the men's suits; and Anna Youle for all her support and assistance.

Suppliers Austin Reed, Church & Co., Compaq, David Clulow Opticians, Elonex, Escada, Filofax, Mucci Bags.

Picture researcher Mariana Sonnenberg; **Picture library assistant** Sam Ward.

PICTURE CREDITS

Key: *b* bottom, *c* centre, *l* left, *r* right, *t* top
Spicers Limited 10*cl*, 30*c/bc*, 31*tl/tr/cl*;
Tony Stone Images jacket front cover *tr*, 4–5, 7*cr*, 21*tr*.

AUTHOR'S BIOGRAPHY

Tim Hindle is founder of the London-based business language consultancy, Working Words, which helps international companies to compose material in English and communicate their messages clearly to their intended audiences. A regular business writer, Tim Hindle has been a contributor to *The Economist* since 1979 and was editor of *EuroBusiness* from 1994 to 1996. As editorial consultant and author, he has produced a number of titles including *Pocket Manager, Pocket MBA*, and *Pocket Finance*, and a biography of Asil Nadir, *The Sultan of Berkeley Square*.